Y0-BRG-582

The School's Role as Moral Authority

R. Freeman Butts, Donald H. Peckenpaugh, and Howard Kirschenbaum, Introduction by Louis J. Rubin

Association for Supervision and Curriculum Development
1701 K St., N.W., Suite 1100
Washington, D.C. 20006

Copyright © 1977 by the Association for Supervision
and Curriculum Development

All rights reserved. No part of this publication may be reproduced
or transmitted in any form or by any means, electronic or mechanical,
including photocopy, recording, or any information storage and retrieval
system, without permission in writing from the publisher.

The materials printed herein are the expressions of the writers and
not necessarily a statement of policy of the Association.

Stock number: 611-77110
Library of Congress Catalog Card Number: 77-89087
ISBN 0-87120-085-6

Contents

ACKNOWLEDGMENTS

Final editing of the manuscript and publication of this booklet were the responsibility of Robert R. Leeper, Associate Director and Editor, ASCD Publications. The production was handled by Patricia Connors, Editorial Assistant, with the assistance of Nancy Olson, Teola T. Jones, and Myra Taub.

Foreword

In Houston, Texas, during the 1977 ASCD Conference, Professor R. Freeman Butts delivered the following remarks and reflections. The occasion was an invited presentation, jointly sponsored by ASCD and the John Dewey Society.

From a base in the social sciences and humanities the author examines tensions between pluralism and civism, between freedom and community focus with particular intensity upon the very idea of public education. He reflects upon implications for schools finding themselves under severe attack from the left and the right and suffering from loss of their one-time role as moral authority.

Philosopher-historian R. Freeman Butts is William F. Russell Professor Emeritus in the Foundations of Education, Teachers College, Columbia University. During the 1976-77 year he served as Visiting Distinguished Professor of Education at San Jose State University while also conducting research into the role of public education in American society.

Both the John Dewey Society and ASCD are privileged to have sponsored this joint meeting at the National Conference. We are further honored to be able to make Professor Butts' thoughts available in this form.

Harold Turner, *Chairperson*
Joint Meeting of the John Dewey Society and
the Association for Supervision and
Curriculum Development

Foreword

[illegible]

Introduction

It is entirely fitting that ASCD has chosen to publish two companion essays on moral education by R. Freeman Butts and Donald Peckenpaugh. Throughout the long history of the Association, it has repeatedly directed attention to the pressing instructional issues of the day. Moral education, whether in the form of values, civics, citizenship, or ethics, has now shifted to center stage. Long an implicit aspect of the curriculum, moral education is destined in the immediate future to become a good deal more explicit and direct. Two factors, mainly, account for this somewhat dramatic change: first, societal events suggest that the traditional provisions for developing a moral citizenry are not entirely adequate; and second, scholarly endeavor has given rise to new, albeit conflicting, theory regarding ethical education.

The essays are complementary. Butts analyzes a number of contradictory arguments regarding values education and demonstrates that there is indeed a legitimate moral authority on which to base the fundamental objectives of schooling. He then goes on to argue, persuasively, that curricular priority should center upon those values at the base of the American civic creed—liberty, equality, and justice. In turn, Peckenpaugh contrasts alternative teaching strategies, reviews a number of ongoing programs, and concludes that a rational approach to moral education need not usurp the role of home or church, prohibit self-determination, or violate the demands of a pluralistic culture.

It is widely assumed that the current need to reinforce ethical education stems from a growing moral decay that has been prompted by the erosion of traditional values. The assumption, however, is not completely valid. To begin with, morality is an abstraction, influenced by changing human conditions that necessitate continuous interpretations and reinterpretations of what is just. There are universals—honesty, integrity, and respect for the rights of others—but these aside, moral behavior is subject to the particular circumstances that prevail. Thus, as we move deeper into a technological era, it becomes increasingly difficult, if not impossible, to transmit an absolute ethical code. Earlier in history, when the rate of social change was considerably slower, a fixed moral system was generally serviceable from one generation to the next. We have now reached the point, however, at which a rapidly developing technocracy and frequent societal realignments require a constant redefinition of moral behavior. The unprecedented expansion of nuclear power and a burgeoning world population, for example, have made it necessary to reconsider a number of long-standing values and beliefs.

Similarly, with the advent of increasing leisure and a larger range of individual autonomy, many of the traditional barriers to unethical conduct have disappeared. When people were obliged to work 80 hours a week to sustain life and when human choices were constrained by limited alternatives, the opportunities for moral turpitude were less abundant. Paradoxically, public education itself has contributed to a propagation of moral dilemmas. The natural consequence of teaching children to think for themselves, to develop inquiring minds, and to speculate about the human predicament is that our ancient prescripts as to what is good and bad must stand the test of rationality. The present generation of youth is inclined to rely heavily, not upon gospel, but upon reason in determining appropriate behavior.

Yet, as both essays note, it is only through education that people become moral. Ethical behavior arises neither out of psychological predisposition nor instinct. Rather, moral quality stems from the cumulative development of appropriate beliefs regarding proper human conduct. The capacity and desire to make ethical decisions—perhaps the major goals of citizenship education—are therefore the product of commitment coupled with choice; one takes certain ideals as moral imperatives and chooses actions that are most likely to fit. In those instances where the ideals are generally embraced, societies facilitate the process by socializing the young in accordance with established codes of behavior. Hence, Professor Butts argues that the public good is best served, not by pluralistic concerns, but by a universal commitment to "the priority of the common civic community."

Happily, the two essays make for a productive marriage in that Butts addresses himself to the substance and basis of moral education, and Peckenpaugh considers its organization and methodology. Both themes, of course, are subject to extraordinary controversy, largely because there is not a definitive consensus as to the purpose of schooling, and because education is widely regarded as having political as well as instructional utility. Amidst all the controversy, however, points of general agreement exist. For example, few persons doubt that schools should directly or indirectly contribute to moral development. ASCD's decision to publish this monograph is in large measure testimony to the growing conviction that the schools must, to an increasing degree, be concerned with moral illiteracy. Similarly, most authorities agree that children, as they mature, pass through progressive levels of emotional and intellectual development. Piaget's celebrated thesis is therefore applicable: Moral reasoning cannot occur until the child is able to deal with abstract ideas; and, its roots take hold when the child turns from a preoccupation with self to a concern about how one's actions affect others.

Ironically, the demand for greater emphasis upon moral-citizenship education has coincided with the press for a "back-to-basics" movement. While opinions differ as to what is basic, the primary thrust of the movement is toward a more cognitive curriculum. Indeed, it is safe to conjecture that the humanistic and affective trends of the past decade are likely to be reversed. The champions of "back-to-basics" appear to have forgotten that there are strong emotional components to moral behavior. In short, people often ignore their ethical senses and behave in irresponsible and immoral ways. Put another way, knowledge is not enough. The individual must both know "what is right" and have the emotional inclination to "do what is right."

Consequently, our critical need is to discover successful procedures through which students can be taught moral concepts in ways that are appropriate to their cognitive and affective maturity. As Peckenpaugh suggests, values clarification and moral analysis techniques offer us a point of departure. The debates regarding the comparative merits of the two methods are regrettable since both, in all probability, have their place. A more significant issue deals with the kinds of professional training essential to teachers. It is not yet clear, for example, whether the training should focus predominantly on teaching procedures or on the intellectual infrastructure of moral judgment.

Another set of issues concerns the countervailing forces in the student's external milieu. What, for instance, can be done to negate the deleterious aspects of television? Are moral infractions, drawn from real-life incidents, fitting topics for classroom analysis? Logic would suggest that the schools cannot successfully advocate moral principles that are not generally reinforced in the society-at-large. It is also difficult to examine ethical and unethical behavior out of context. Two boys, for example, may be habitual petty thieves. If, however, one steals out of need and the other out of alienation or hostility, different sorts of correctives may be required. Finally, we must recognize that moral humans come in diverse forms: There are different bases of moral determination; alternative systems of reasoning can be used; and moral judgments often depend upon the vagaries of the particular situation.

Perhaps of greatest consequence, it is impossible to teach values and ethical beliefs outside the framework of the learner's emotional makeup. What constitutes a successful teaching strategy with one child, therefore, may prove quite unsuccessful with another. Thus the principles of individualization are also relevant.

The reader is likely to find much for thought in the two essays that follow. They are informative as well as provocative, rich in detail, and of unquestionable benefit to the profession.

Louis J. Rubin
Professor of Education
University of Illinois, Urbana

* Editor's note: The third paper in this booklet, "Values Education: 1976 and Beyond" by Howard Kirschenbaum, was added after this introduction was written and after the initial stages of publication. We recommend this paper to our readership because of its timeliness and because it extends the discussion of the topic covered by this publication.

The Public School as Moral Authority

R. Freeman Butts

Until almost yesterday the public school was a fixed article of faith in the American public creed, commanding powerful moral authority as a national unifier, liberator, and equalizer. For a long time public education has had persuasive moral as well as legal authority behind it. At various times in the past the public school has drawn upon the political authority of the founders of the Republic, the religious authority of nondenominational Protestantism, the work ethic of middle class virtues, the academic authority of literacy and knowledge in an education-oriented society, the cohesive authority of assimilator and Americanizer in an immigrant-flooded society, and the socializing authority as agent of progressive reform in a rapidly modernizing and industrializing society.

But for a decade or so the erosion of the legitimacy of some of the major institutions in American society has begun to effect the "deauthorization" of the public school as well, that is, its moral authority to act as a guide or leader in social affairs has been seriously questioned and weakened. At the end of our 200th year as a nation, the value of public education is being attacked from several quarters, and the American people are engaged in searching anew for the

* Presented at a joint session of the Association for Supervision and Curriculum Development and the John Dewey Society at the ASCD Conference, Houston, Texas, March 20, 1977. Based on and adapted from the final chapter of a forthcoming book by Professor Butts: R. Freeman Butts. *American Public Education: From Revolution to Reform, 1776-1976*. New York: Holt, Rinehart and Winston, 1978. Used by permission of the publisher.

legitimate authority for education in the future. The question now is what sort of community most appropriately gives legitimacy to the goals of education in general and to public education in particular. I would like to deal with two major approaches to this question. The first says that the authority for education should rest with a number of pluralistic communities; the second says the authority should reside in the political or civic community. In oversimplified but useful terms, the two general approaches to the moral authority of public education may be identified as pluralism and civism.

Pluralists seek moral authority and legitimacy for education in the many different communities that serve to bind individuals and groups together on the basis of religious, racial, ethnic, linguistic, cultural, or local cohesion and unity. They see such positive values in diversity and variety of pluralistic associations that they consider them to be the essence of community around which education and schooling should cluster. Some pluralists are exceedingly critical of public education for being so conformist in outlook and practice, recommending that public schools should emphasize ethnic studies, multicultural studies, bilingual studies, and in general should reflect the enormous diversity of their respective cultural communities. Other pluralists see no special authority in public education, viewing it as no more legitimate or authoritative than private schools or any number of other educative agencies, such as the family, churches, and voluntary associations of all kinds. Still others view public education as positively *illegitimate,* because of its historic connection with an exploitative, capitalist, corporate liberal state.

By contrast, "civicists" or "citizenists" seek the principal authority and legitimacy for public education in the democratic civic or political community.[1] They argue that public education has a special responsibility for being a positive force in promoting the values, the

[1] Though not often found in current usage, the word "civicist" I derive from civics (the study of government) as physicist is derived from physics. In fact, however, the words "civism" and "civicism" are perfectly good, but seldom used, English words, included in both Webster's Unabridged Dictionary (Second Edition) and the Oxford English Dictionary. "Civism" is taken from the French *"civisme"* (taken in turn from the Latin "civis" meaning citizen), which the French coined to refer to the devotion or well-affected disposition toward the new nation they established in their Revolution of 1789. In English, the word "civism" refers generally to the "citizen principle" as envisioned in the ancient

knowledge, and the skills of participation required for maintaining and improving the democratic political community and for strengthening the freedom, the equality, the justice, and the popular consent promised by the Declaration of Independence, the Constitution, and the Bill of Rights. For these values to provide protection for the diversity of pluralist associations, they must be held in common by all the pluralisms or else privatism, contention, and conflict may threaten the welfare of all but the most powerful groups in the society.

The "New Pluralists"

Despite the origins of the term "cultural pluralism" in the early part of the twentieth century, the term has not been in widespread professional or popular use until its rather sudden and popular rebirth in the 1960's. For a decade or so, it has become exceedingly popular in the hands of a number of different critics of public education. I can mention only three examples. They are representative of (a) new ethnicists, (b) a neo-conservative movement in political philosophy, and (c) a variety of critics in educational philosophy and policy who espouse pluralism both from within and outside the educational establishment.

Heartened by the success of blacks in the civil rights movement of the 1960's but frustrated by the feeling that similar forms of discrimination continued to apply to the descendants of white immigrants, a new and sometimes fierce pride in ethnic traditions has appeared both in professional and popular literature and has reappeared as a lively political force in the elections of the 1960's and 1970's. Books and articles by Michael Novak, formerly on the staff of the Rockefeller Foundation, Nathan Glazer and Daniel Patrick Moynihan of Harvard, and Rev. Andrew Greeley, Director of the

---

Greek and Roman republics, especially referring to the tradition of self-sacrifice for the public good. It came then by extension to mean in general the principles of good citizenship. Civism is a useful single shorthand term for the longer phrase "principles of good citizenship in a republic." It connotes the need for building a sense of cohesion that will bind citizens together into a viable political community. Civicism is defined in *Webster's New International Dictionary of the English Language* as "principles of civil government" or "devotion, adherence, or conformity, to civic principles or to the duties and rights belonging to civic government."

Center for the Study of Pluralism at the University of Chicago, became well-known.[2]

The new ethnicity is defined by Novak as:

> . . . a movement of self-knowledge on the part of members of the third and fourth generations of southern and eastern European immigrants in the U.S. In a broader sense, the new ethnicity includes a renewed self-consciousness on the part of other generations and other ethnic groups: the Irish, the Norwegians and Swedes, the Germans, the Chinese and Japanese, and others . . . .[3]

Novak argues for the introduction of ethnic studies into the public school curriculum as follows:

> With even modest adjustments in courses in history, literature, and the social sciences, material can be introduced that illuminates inherited patterns of family life, values, and preferences. The purpose of introducing multicultural materials is neither chauvinistic nor propagandistic but realistic. Education ought to illuminate what is happening in the self of each child.[4]

The demand for ethnic heritage studies and multicultural studies in the public schools has arisen from views and sentiments like those of Novak. Another approach arising from the new ethnicity argues that "ethnic" *schools* would be better than common public schools. Andrew Greeley implies this when he argues that an "ethnic miracle" has been achieved by some of the immigrant groups in rising out of poverty, hatred, and discrimination by their own efforts and in spite of the public schools. In fact, their own parochial schools aided Irish Catholics, Italians, and Poles to achieve financial success and middle class status in a matter of a few decades from their arrival in the United States. The public high school did not assist in this

[2] See, for example, Michael Novak. *The Rise of the Unmeltable Ethnics.* New York: Macmillan, 1972; Nathan Glazer and Daniel Patrick Moynihan. *Beyond the Melting Pot.* Cambridge, Massachusetts: M.I.T. Press, 1963; Lawrence H. Fuchs, editor. *American Ethnic Politics.* New York: Harper and Row, 1968; Edgar Litt. *Ethnic Politics in America.* Glenview, Illinois: Scott Foresman, 1970; Andrew W. Greeley. *Why Can't They Be Like Us?* New York: American Jewish Committee, 1968; and Peter Schrag. *The Decline of the WASP.* New York: Simon and Schuster, 1971.

[3] Michael Novak. "The New Ethnicity." *The Center Magazine,* July/Aug. 1974. p. 18.

[4] *Ibid.,* p. 25.

process because the immigrants' financial success came *before* they began to flock to schools. Their success was due to their family life, their hard work, their ambition, their courage, their work ethic, and their sacrifice. They were given no favors and no help, but they *were* given personal freedom and the chance to turn their hard work into economic progress.

The hint for social policy in all this is that public funds should go to aid ethnic schools that have been so important in the "ethnic miracle" of the past:

> . . . *one might take it as a tentative hypothesis that the school is a rather poor institution for facilitating the upward mobility of minority groups—until they first acquire some kind of rough income parity.* The naive American faith that equality of education produces equality of income seems to have been stood on its head in the case of the ethnics. For them, better income meant more effective education.
>
> Nor did the public schools play the critical "Americanization" role that such educators as Dr. James B. Conant expected them to play in the 1940's and 1950's. Even taking into account parents' education and income, the most successful of the ethnics—educationally, occupationally, and economically—went to parochial schools, and they did so at a time when the schools were even more crowded than they are today, staffed by even less adequately trained teachers, and administered by an even smaller educational bureaucracy than the very small one that somehow manages to keep the parochial schools going today. Again: a social policy hint: Maybe what matters about schools for a minority group is, as my colleague Professor William McCready has remarked, that they are "our" schools (whoever "we" may be).[5]

A second fountainhead for the new pluralism springs from a variety of political analyses in the fields of moral and political philosophy in which fundamental questions are being raised concerning the future of the institution of public education itself and more broadly the whole range of institutions that make up liberal democratic government in America.

It seems clear that during the early 1970's there has been a growing conservative reaction against the educational and social reform efforts of the 1960's. One could cite Robert Nisbet of Columbia in

[5] Andrew M. Greeley. "The Ethnic Miracle.' *The Public Interest,* No. 45, Fall 1976. p. 29. See also: Greeley. *The American Catholic; a Social Portrait.* New York: Basic Books, 1977.

historical sociology, Robert Nozick of Harvard in political philosophy, Milton Friedman of Chicago in economics, and Harvard's Nathan Glazer in education and social structure.

These scholars call for the reassertion of the values of private freedoms, individual rights, the free market mechanism, the minimal state, the free play of voluntary groups, mutual aid associations, and reinforcement of pluralistic racial and social groupings of all kinds. Along with the positive values to be associated with freedom for the 100 flowers to bloom, goes an attack upon the overweening welfare state, the inquisitional and repressive measures of the bureaucracies, the leviathan mentality, and a general disenchantment with the liberal welfare state and its policies.

Let me give just one example of the new conservatism. Robert Nisbet begins by saying:

> I believe the single most remarkable fact at the present time in the West is neither technological nor economic, but *political*: the waning of the historic political community, the widening sense of the obsolescence of politics as a civilized pursuit, even as a habit of mind. By political community I mean more than the legal state. I have in mind the whole fabric of rights, liberties, participants, and protections that has been even above industrialism, I think, the dominant element of modernity in the West . . . .
>
> We are witnessing . . . a gathering revolt . . . against the whole structure of wealth, privilege, and power that the contemporary democratic state has come to represent.[6]

Nisbet's prescriptions for the restoration of authority are to recover the central values of social and cultural pluralism rather than political cohesion and to revive the prestige of the private as contrasted with the public. In briefest terms, Nisbet defines four central values of pluralism. Correctly understood, (a) it preserves functional autonomy of major social institutions (avoiding intrusion of the state into the spheres of school, university, family, and religion); (b) it decentralizes power into as many hands as possible; (c) it recognizes that hierarchy and stratification of function and role are unavoidable and honorable and to be preserved from intrusion by the arbitrary power of regulatory agencies in the "name of a vain and

[6] Robert Nisbet. *Twilight of Authority*. New York: Oxford University Press, 1975. pp. 3-5.

vapid equality"; and (d) it relies as much as possible upon informal custom, folkway, spontaneous tradition—sanctioned habits of mind—rather than formal law, ordinance, or administrative regulation.

Thus, Nisbet argues for the renascence in education of pluralism, privatism, kinship, localism, and voluntary association. For example, regarding kinship, it was a great mistake of the democratic dogma to think that political institutions like the public school could do better than the family in the realm of education. Regarding localism, the opposition to busing springs from pride of attachment to neighborhood rather than from racism. Regarding voluntary association, the prime agents of human accomplishment are the intimate, free, relevant, and spontaneous associations of self-help and mutual aid, the best illustration of such laissez-faire phenomena being Milton Friedman's proposal for educational vouchers. In other words, private schools under the auspices of churches, labor unions, cooperatives, neighborhoods, and families have been notably less expensive and more efficient than public schools:

> From what labyrinths of bureaucracy we would be saved in the grim worlds of social workers and educational administrators had there been instituted in the beginning a system [of education] whereby a natural, already existing social group—the household—would be the means of distributing public funds for welfare and for education.[7]

In the concluding paragraphs of his book, Nisbet argues that it all comes down to the way we conceive the nature of citizenship:

> If there is to be a citizenship in the useful sense of that word, it must have its footings in the groups, associations, and localities in which we actually spend our lives—not in the abstract and now bankrupt idea of *patrie,* as conceived by the Jacobins and their descendants.[8]

If the signposts of the future are the upthrusts of ethnicity, localism, regionalism, religion, and kinship, this is exactly what we had 200 years ago when the framers of the American commonwealth sought to overcome these very pluralistic elements in the founding of a political community and a constitutional order whose motto became *"E Pluribus Unum."* And Nisbet's notions of private education based upon these same elements of traditional pluralism were

[7] *Ibid.,* p. 278.
[8] *Ibid.,* p. 286.

exactly the characteristics of the schools and colleges of the colonial period that the founders and their successors sought to replace by their proposals for a public education that would be universal, free, common, and eventually secular and compulsory.

A third source of pluralism has focused critical attention directly upon the practices, the philosophy, and the policies of the public schools. One line of reasoning, often summed up under the heading of the "romantic critics," has led to the radical conclusion that the public school system cannot be reclaimed and should be replaced by voluntary efforts of many kinds. Another argument has led to proposals for "alternatives" to loosen up and introduce flexibility into the public system itself. These two refrains became dominant themes of the educational discussions of the 1960's and 1970's.

Henry Perkinson, educational historian at New York University, accurately sums up the essence of the romantic critics:

> One after another the romantic critics have uncovered layers of authoritarianism in our educational arrangements. To a man they reject imposition and advocate a child-centered or learner-centered education. The smorgasbord curriculum of John Holt, the inquiry method of Postman and Weingartner, the open classroom of Herbert Kohl, the free school of George Dennison, the learning web of Ivan Illich—all point to an educational process where people learn what, how, and when they like.[9]

The embracing of pluralism in education can scarcely go further. The specific concern for political community is hardly in evidence except for a minor refrain of somehow removing the evils of a capitalist system. The overall impact of the romantic critics is probably much more important, though less direct, than often admitted by the educational establishment.

A second kind of educational pluralism, that which emanates from within the establishment and focuses upon reform of the public schools in the direction of greater alternatives, reflects much of the orientation if not the fire and outrage of the romantics. Philosophers of education, educational policy advisers, national commissions, federal programs, and national association projects begin to echo if not

[9] Henry S. Perkinson. *Two Hundred Years of American Educational Thought*. New York: David McKay, 1976. pp. 307-08. For an excellent brief bibliography of the major writings of the romantic critics, see: pp. 310-12.

incorporate the pluralistic criticisms that have reverberated through the press and other mass media for over a decade.

Philosophy of education, which had been socially oriented to the ideals of democracy as well as individual development in the spirit of John Dewey's pragmatism and experimentalism through most of the period from the late 1920's to the early 1950's, began to be absorbed by linguistic analysis of philosophical problems in much of the1950's and early 1960's. Then it began to rediscover the individualistic and pluralistic side of Dewey's philosophy and especially that of Horace Kallen, who is generally conceded to be the father of the term "cultural pluralism."[10] The essence of the idea is that primary human associations are the most basic communities consisting of natural affinities and sentiments. The individual can most readily develop the potentials of his personality and self-fulfillment in and through such associations. A genuine pluralist society will thus honor and encourage the diversity of the natural primary groups based upon kinship, language, religion, culture, and locality. Education should therefore recognize and encourage such diverse loyalties, both as the essence of democracy and of personal development. Obviously, this revival of the philosophy of cultural pluralism fits nicely with the rise of the new ethnicity and a nonauthoritarian political philosophy whether stemming from conservative, liberal, or radical sources.

Some philosophers and practitioners of education, imbued with the pluralistic emphasis upon individual and primary group attachment, argue that the public schools should stress the pluralistic character of American society through multicultural studies. Others find a greatly reduced or nonexistent place for public education as it has been historically developed. One of the most forthright statements from within philosophy of education is that of Seymour Itzkoff of Smith College, whose recent book entitled *A New Public Education* finds a large place for private voluntary effort and little for a public

[10] See, for example: Horace M. Kallen. *Culture and Democracy in the United* States. New York: Boni & Liveright, 1924; William Greenbaum. "America in Search of a New Ideal: an Essay on the Rise of Pluralism." *Harvard Educational Review* 4 (3); August 1974; several articles in *Philosophy of Education 1976: Proceedings of the Thirty-Second Annual Meeting of the Philosophy of Education Society*. Urbana, Illinois: *Educational Theory,* 1976; Charles A. Tesconi, Jr. *Schooling in America; A Social Philosophical Perspective*. Boston: Houghton Mifflin, 1975. Part IV; and Thomas F. Green. *Education and Pluralism: Ideal and Reality*. Syracuse, New York: Syracuse University, 1966.

governmental role in education. *His* conception of the "new public education" is so new that it really means private education.

Calling to witness Horace Kallen, John Dewey, Thomas Green, and George Dennison, Itzkoff argues that the local autonomous cultural community is the natural context and authority for education. He argues that the educational system can be reformed by a gradual shift to voluntarism and eventually a full voucher system. In this way, the stagnant, bureaucratized, politicized public system can be given over to those who will be the ultimate beneficiaries; parents and children will have maximum opportunity to realize their value commitments in a wholly voluntary system of community-based schooling.

Itzkoff concludes that the legitimacy of the public school and the moral authority it once had have been irretrievably lost, confounded at least in part by the new stress on an aggressive equality by fiat, forced integration, affirmative action, and proliferation of quotas enforced by the intercession of government:

> The traumas that the schools have recently undergone have arisen precisely because of our waning confidence in the school. The moral consensus that undergirded the public school for so many decades has dissolved. And in its absence the state schools have fallen prey to a host of political locusts. Drained of its integrity, public education has become an automatic target for every new political grab. This has caused many thoughtful people to abandon hope for the public school as a functioning national institution in its traditional moral as well as skill-training role.[11]

In place of the *common* public school would arise a pluralism of voluntary schools around which individuals with similar values, social concerns, and cultural ideals would cluster. Itzkoff opts for unregulated vouchers so that the greatest kind of differentiation (except racial) could lead to schools based on special interests, special talents, special cultural and ethnic orientations, and specialized admission policies:

> Free choice is the key, the right to be taught by whom one chooses, and the right to teach only those one feels will benefit from one's skills.[12]

[11] Seymour Itzkoff. *A New Public Education*. New York: David McKay Company, Inc., 1976. pp. 333-34.

[12] *Ibid.*, p. 356.

Now it is still too early to record the disappearance of the public school as Itzkoff proposes, but prominent voices on the policy scene are giving notice that its role and importance should be viewed as greatly curtailed. Only one or two examples can be cited.

In his policy pronouncements summarized in his book *Public Education,* historian Lawrence A. Cremin, president of Teachers College, notes that one of the failings of the progressive theory of education was that it focused too exclusively on the public schools as agencies of social reform and thus ignored the possibilities of other educative institutions. In his chapter on "Public Education and the Education of the Public," Cremin puts his policy observations this way:

> The fact is that the public is educated by many institutions, some of them private and some of them public, and that public schools are only one among several important public institutions that educate the public. There are, after all, public libraries, public museums, public television, and public work projects (the most extensive of which are the military services) . . . .[13]

Cremin does not flagellate the public schools as many other pluralists do, but his thesis is that they are only one among many educative agencies, and thus apparently they have no special primacy of place in a democratic society and no distinctive purpose that other educative agencies cannot fulfill.

> In sum, then, to think comprehensively about education we must consider policies with respect to a wide variety of institutions that educate, not only schools and colleges, but libraries, museums, day-care centers, radio and television stations, offices, factories, and farms. To be concerned solely with schools, given the educational world we live in today, is to have a kind of fortress mentality in contending with a very fluid and dynamic situation.[14]

Though public schools are not specifically denigrated in Cremin's views, they come off diminished in importance in comparison with all the other educative agencies he mentions. I would ask which of these have as their *primary* purpose the formation of good citizens? Cremin does not propose priorities in this fashion. He seems

[13] Lawrence A. Cremin. *Public Education.* New York: Basic Books, 1976. p. 58.

[14] *Ibid.,* p. 59.

simply to be asking for public debate about the alternatives. His view lends itself in *other* hands to a reification of "alternatives" as the be-all and end-all of educational policy.

One such policy position was taken recently by Theodore R. Sizer, former Dean of the Harvard Graduate School of Education, who argued for a pluralism of educational institutions as the best solution for the future. He acknowledged that he had particularly been influenced by Cremin's *Public Education,* Tyack's *One Best System,* Glazer's *Affirmative Discrimination,* and Glazer and Moynihan's *Ethnicity.* Sizer's policy proposals are threefold. First, they do not simply reassert that the public schools are the one best system:

> . . . the sooner those responsible for public education recognize that nonpublic schools, the so-called deschooling movement, the alternative education movement, and the advocates of neighborhood community schools all in their several ways represent a new reality in American educational politics, so much the better for the children. It is no surprise that efforts at a national unified teachers union have lost momentum and the political interest for increased federal involvement in the "improvement" of education has slowed. Disaggregation is a policy with new adherents. One need only look at the growing edge of the curricula of teacher training institutions to see the interest in alternatives and in the special educational needs of special groups, increasingly ethnic as well as racial groups. The *common* school, the single institution built around a common American creed, never was and clearly never will be.[15]

A second pluralistic injunction from Sizer rests on Cremin's argument that the part that *schools* can play in the education of children is limited. In fact, he goes so far as to acknowledge that Cremin's message on configurations of education will serve to bury the public school:

> Cremin would include, along with the school, the church, the family, and the ethnic group. *The times are ready for a new kind of pluralism in schooling,* a pluralism which relates the schools with other institutions in carefully contrived and thoughtfully constructed ways. Cremin's "Public Education" drives the final nail into the coffin of the late-nineteenth century nativist creation of a "one best system." The sooner that the educa-

[15] Theodore Ryland Sizer. "Education and Assimilation: A Fresh Plea for Pluralism." *Phi Delta Kappan,* September 1976. p. 34.

tional establishment at large recognizes this, the better (again) for the children.[16]

Sizer is not worried about the segregative aspects of alternative schools. He believes that the "thread of nationhood" and social cohesion will be adequately served by the much more powerful mass media. He is apparently willing to leave the "common thread of nationhood" to Walter Cronkite, Harry Reasoner, and Ann Landers. So, he comes to his third proposal that youngsters could well divide their time between different kinds of schools: ethnic schools, community schools, regional schools, yes, even "national schools." His final message is that there should be multiple opportunities for all children and parents to choose complementary institutions, a smorgasbord of schools.

All in all, then, whether it came from outside or from inside the education establishment, the call for "alternatives" has become one of the most popular terms in the educational lexicon of the 1970's. It has been applied to all manner of undertakings, from well thought-out programs to almost any kind of improvisation that will take bored, restless, or disruptive youth off the backs of embattled and harassed public school administrators and teachers. Several national commissions have tried to tackle the problem, and in its way the federal government has responded to the political interests of particular target groups including the Teacher Corps for the disadvantaged, the Bilingual Act for those with limited English, and the Ethnic Heritage Act for special ethnic groups. Above all, major professional groups have taken up the call for multicultural studies with enthusiasm.

An example of the enthusiastic embracing of multicultural education and cultural pluralism is that of the American Association of Colleges for Teacher Education, which appointed its Multicultural Education Commission in February 1971 and officially adopted its statement entitled "No One Model American" at its Board of Directors meeting in November 1972. The statement is quoted here at length to indicate its strong attachment to the philosophy of cultural pluralism:

> Multicultural education is education which values cultural pluralism. Multicultural education rejects the view that schools should seek to

[16] *Ibid.*, p. 34.

melt away cultural differences or the view that schools should merely tolerate cultural pluralism. Instead, multicultural education affirms that schools should be oriented toward the cultural enrichment of all children and youth through programs rooted to the preservation and extension of cultural diversity as a fact of life in American society, and it affirms that this cultural diversity is a valuable resource that should be preserved and extended. It affirms that major education institutions should strive to preserve and enhance cultural pluralism.[17]

A careful reading of the full AACTE statement will reveal not only the obvious concern for the pluralistic communities, but also virtually no reference to the common elements that bind the different groups together. In this respect, AACTE and many other enthusiastic adopters of multicultural education have forgotten or little noticed a major tenet that the father of cultural pluralism always insisted upon—the fundamental principles of *political* democracy that must underlie the diversities of *cultural* pluralism. Horace Kallen always insisted that it was only upon this foundation that:

> . . . the outlines of a possibily great and truly democratic commonwealth become discernible. Its form would be that of the federal republic; its substance a democracy of nationalities, cooperating voluntarily and autonomously through common institutions in the enterprise of self-realization through the perfection of men according to their kind. The common language of the commonwealth, the language of its great tradition, would be English, but each nationality would have for its emotional and involuntary life its own peculiar dialect or speech, its own individual and inevitable esthetic and intellectual forms. The political and economic life of the commonwealth is a single unit and serves as the foundation and background for the realization of the distinctive individuality of each *nation* that composes it and of the pooling of these in a harmony above them all. Thus, "American civilization' may come to mean the perfection of the cooperative harmonies of "European civilization"—the waste, the squalor, and the distress of Europe being eliminated—a multiplicity in a unity, an orchestration of mankind.[18]

When Kallen came to identify the "common institutions" funda-

[17] William A. Hunter, editor. *Multicultural Education Through Competency-Based Teacher Education*. Washington, D.C.: American Association of Colleges for Teacher Education, 1974. p. 21. See also: for example, "Alternative Approaches to Teacher Education." *Journal of Teacher Education*, Jan./Feb., 1977.

[18] Horace M. Kallen. *Culture and Democracy in the United States*. New York: Boni and Liveright, 1924. p. 124.

mental to the political commonwealth, he always gave primacy to the public schools. He was opposed to separate schools for separate cultural groups except as supplementary and voluntary additions to the public schools, which he urged all to attend. He opposed the injection of pluralistic religion into the public schools and he opposed public support for private or ethnic schools. In 1956, when he defined the elements of the "American Bible" that summed up the common creed of all Americans, he included not only the Declaration of Independence; the Constitution; and the great credos of Washington, Jefferson, Madison, Lincoln, Wilson, Holmes, Brandeis, F. D. Roosevelt, Truman, and the Supreme Court on separation of church and state, but also Horace Mann's Twelfth Report to the Massachusetts Board of Education.[19]

Kallen's faith in the political commonwealth of democracy and in the common public school as the foundation for the maintenance and flourishing of the cultural pluralisms that should cooperate in its support could put him in the list of advocates of civism as well as of pluralism. The same could be said of John Dewey in reverse fashion. Though it is popular to call upon Dewey as well as Kallen in support of pluralism, as Cremin and Itzkoff and others have done, it is also true that Dewey's *political* philosophy stresses the importance of the meaning of the Public as the key to the building of a Great Community along with the importance of the smaller face-to-face communities in nourishing pluralism.

The New Civism

In the 1920's the excessively individualistic and pluralistic character of American society led John Dewey to be concerned about recapturing the meaning of the public, just as the nativist drive for assimilation led Horace Kallen to be concerned about revitalizing the meaning of cultural and ethnic pluralism. In his lectures on "The Public and Its Problems" at Kenyon College in 1926, just fifty years before the bicentennial year, Dewey was especially concerned about the search for conditions under which the Great Society could become the Great Community. Modern science, technology, and industrialization had created a Great Society characterized by large-scale

[19] Horace M. Kallen. *Cultural Pluralism and the American Idea; An Essay in Social Philosophy*. Philadelphia: University of Pennsylvania Press, 1956. p. 87.

associated or joint activity and aggregated collective action, but what was needed was a Great Community that would be not simply physical and organic but characterized by a communal life that is moral, emotionally, intellectually, and consciously sustained. No amount of merely aggregated collective action of itself constitutes a community. Dewey found the essence of community in the generic social sense of democracy nourished by intelligence and education.[20]

The key to realizing consciousness of community is through revivifying and vitalizing an organized, articulate Public. His meaning of the public goes something like this: Human acts have consequences upon others; perception of these consequences leads to efforts to control action so as to secure *some* consequences and *not* others. Consequences of actions are of two kinds: (a) those that only affect the persons directly engaged in a transaction are private; (b) those that affect others beyond those immediately concerned are public. The effort to regulate these indirect consequences and care for the welfare of others is the realm of the public:

> The public consists of all those who are affected by the indirect consequences of transactions to such an extent that it is deemed necessary to have those consequences systematically cared for. Officials are those who look for and take care of the interests thus affected.[21]

Significantly, Dewey argued that this supervision and regulation of the consequences of actions by individuals and by groups cannot be accomplished by the primary groups themselves. It is just such consequences that call the public into being. The public organized to conduct these affairs through officials is the state. When the association known as the public takes on the task of regulating the conjoint actions of individuals and groups, the public becomes a political state or political community. Among the major characteristics of a state or political community are not only a temporal or geographic location and organized political institutions like legislatures and courts, but a special care for children and other dependents who are looked upon as peculiarly its wards:

> In the degree, then, that a certain measure of instruction and training is deemed to have significant consequences for the social body, rules

[20] John Dewey. *The Public and Its Problems.* New York: Holt, 1927. p. 149. (Swallow Press, 1954).

[21] *Ibid.*, p. 16.

are laid down affecting the action of parents in relation to their children, and those who are not parents are taxed—Herbert Spencer to the contrary notwithstanding—to maintain schools.[22]

The significance of a representative democracy is that every citizen-voter and especially every teacher is an "officer of the public," a representative of the public as much as an elected official. So every citizen has a dual capacity as a private person and as an officer of the public. The essential meaning of a representative democracy is so to organize its affairs that the public good dominates the private interest. Herein lies the significance of public schools in contrast to private schools—to develop the "officer of the public" role of all individuals and to aid them to enhance their political roles on behalf of the public good.

This concern by Dewey for a search for political community strengthened the recurrent calls for "education for democracy" that infused the thought of social frontiersmen from the 1930's to the 1950's, as exemplified in the works of George S. Counts, John L. Childs, R. Bruce Raup, Harold Rugg, and their associates and students. But the mood of democratic social reform and the search for a community of persuasion went out of style among philosophers of education and among much of the entire profession during the 1950's and 1960's. Eventually, however, the experiences of the Vietnam War, the campus unrest with its attendant changes in values, and the constitutional crisis swirling around the Watergate struggles pointed in two directions: an increased cynicism and alienation with regard to political affairs; and a marked revival of concern for deliberate education in the public schools that would help to bring closer to realization the stated values of the democratic political community.

Almost all the polls and observers since the early 1970's continued to document the decline of respect for the legitimacy and moral authority of the political system. The percentage of voter turnout dropped steadily in each election from 1960 to 1976 when only 53 percent voted, with especially low concentrations of people under 30, the poor, the less well-educated, and blue collar workers. It was estimated that two-thirds of those between 18 and 21 did not vote, and over half of those between 21 and 29 did not vote. Although there was not the massive failure to vote in 1976 that some had pre-

[22] *Ibid.*, p. 63.

dicted, there was evident a widespread sense of powerlessness among voters and even more so among nonvoters.[23]

The changing values of youth, the polls tell us, show not only a lessening of respect for established institutions as guides for moral behavior and decline in patriotism, but a rise in privatism and greater preoccupation with self at the expense of devoting one's self to family or community.[24]

These attitudes go along with the reports of surveys of political knowledge achieved by high school students. The National Assessment of Educational Progress has documented in great detail the status of political knowledge among 13-year-olds and 17-year-olds. The fairly flat conclusion from test surveys of citizenship made in 1969-70 and social studies in 1971-72 was:

> Young Americans lack knowledge of the fundamentals of politics and civil rights.[25]

A preliminary report on the second round of achievement tests conducted in the school year 1975-76 found little cause for encouragement.[26] Apparently there has not been massive improvement in the teaching of the social studies since the shortcomings of most civic education in the schools were aptly appraised by the Committee on Pre-Collegiate Education of the American Political Science Association in 1971:

> (It) transmits a naive, unrealistic, and romanticized image of political life which confuses the ideals of democracy with the realities of politics . . . .[27]

On the positive side, there *has* been an upsurge of effort to focus the civic instruction of the schools upon problems of civil rights of

[23] Report of a poll by *The New York Times* and CBS in *The Times,* November 16, 1976.

[24] Daniel Yankelovich. *The New Morality: A Profile of American Youth in the Seventies.* New York: McGraw-Hill, 1974.

[25] Education Commission of the States. *National Assessment Achievements: Findings, Interpretations and Uses.* Report #48. Denver, Colorado, June 1974. p. 1. See also: N.A.E.P. *Newsletter,* December 1973 and January-February 1974. Details are contained in N.A.E.P. Report 03-85-01. *Political Knowledge and Attitudes,* December 1973.

[26] National Assessment of Educational Progress reported in *The New York Times,* January 2, 1977.

[27] APSA *Newsletter,* Summer 1971.

ethnic minorities, women, and youth; the basic concepts of law and justice; the Constitution and Bill of Rights; and the realities of the political process.

Fortunately, elementary and secondary school educators are beginning to think seriously about citizenship education again, and they are beginning to do something about it. Within a short time we shall have a report on basic principles and practices from the National Task Force on Citizenship Education, sponsored by the Danforth Foundation and the Kettering Foundation.[28] Two aspects of the renewal of interest in civic education are especially impressive to me.

In the 1970's, projects under the heading of "law-related education" have been snowballing under the assiduous leadership of several new organizations and old foundations that have been encouraging the joint efforts of social science scholars, practicing teachers, and representatives of the legal, justice, and education professions. Some of these projects are described in a 1975 publication of the Constitutional Rights Foundation. Norman Gross and Charles White of the American Bar Association's Special Committee on Youth Education for Citizenship summarized the recent rapid development as follows:

> In 1971, statewide programs were being organized or were under headway in only six states. Now (1975), 26 states have at least incipient statewide projects. In 1971, no more than 150 law-related education projects were active in the schools. Today, there are almost 400.
>
> Curriculum materials have multiplied dramatically in the past decade.[29]

Especially impressive is the project on Law in a Free Society (Santa Monica, California), which is drawing up lesson plans, case books, course outlines, teachers' guides, and multimedia instructional materials on eight basic concepts that should pervade a comprehensive curriculum in civic education from kindergarten through the twelfth grade: four concepts stress civism (authority, justice, participation, and responsibility; and four stress pluralism (freedom,

[28] National Task Force on Citizenship Education. *Education for Responsible Citizenship*. New York: McGraw-Hill, 1977.

[29] Law, Education, and Participation. *Education for Law and Justice: Whose Responsibility—A Call for National Action*. Los Angeles: Constitutional Rights Foundation, 1975. pp. 46-47.

privacy, diversity, and property). The project asserts that these are the fundamental ideas necessary for the understanding of a free polity and should be the core of study in civic education. Such concepts could fruitfully bring to life the values, knowledge, and practice in real-life experiences that must go together in an efficacious civic education.

Another pedagogical movement that has gained widespread attention among professionals as well as the public has been the renewed interest in the "teaching of values." Of special significance for civic education is the work of Lawrence Kohlberg at Harvard, which is now being applied to civic education programs in schools in Cambridge and Brookline, Massachusetts, under the direction of Kohlberg and Ralph Mosher and in the Pittsburgh area under the direction of Edwin Fenton at Carnegie-Mellon.[30] The work, based on a theory of six stages of moral/cognitive development, has caused considerable stir in psychological and philosophical circles.

In the first two stages, people are found to think and act on the traditional bases of fear of punishment, desire for reward, or exchange of favors. In the middle two stages, they think and act on the conventional bases devoted to maintaining the political and social order by meeting the expectations held out for them or duties imposed upon them by authorities for the sake of the good of the order. In the upper two stages, people think and act on the basis of moral principles genuinely accepted by the individual rather than on the basis of simply conforming to the authority of the group. Stage 5 is the stage of the social contract and human rights (for example, the Declaration of Independence and the U.S. Constitution), and Stage 6 is the stage of universal ethical principles pertaining to liberty, equality, and justice. The Kohlberg theory and experimentation over several years argue that the most effective teaching of values can be undertaken by direct confrontation of moral decisions in open discussions between teachers and students. Such a process, conducted in the setting of a just community, will move students from lower levels to higher stages of development.

So the Kohlberg approach means that if the vast *majority* of American youths are ever to reach the higher stages represented by the Declaration of Independence and the Bill of Rights, then a civic

[30] See *Social Education* 40 (4) ; April 1976.

education must include the deliberate effort to develop a civic morality among all high school and college students. Not simply "clarifying one's values," not simply acquiring a breadth of political knowledge, not simply acquaintance with the history and structure of government in the past. If we are to continue to have mass secondary and higher education, there should be a common civic core to it. If we are to continue to have a democratic political community, the schools must give priority to their civic task.

Thus, it has become evident to me that a revival of an appropriate civic role for public education is inevitably linked with the vitality of the public schools themselves as a major force in American life. Can they serve the values of the political community devoted to freedom and equality and justice, and still serve the values of the several pluralistic communities? Here the evidence again is ambiguous. Has the constant drumbeat of attack upon the idea as well as the practices of public schools so undermined faith in them that they cannot be a vital force in revitalizing the future of the liberal democratic political institutions that have nurtured them and that they were originally designed to serve?

As I view the search for purpose in American public education over the past fifty or sixty years, I would sum it up this way: freedom in education has been enhanced; equality has been pursued with some success; and a sense of community has been diminished. Compared with a half-century ago, freedom for parents, children, and teachers as expressed in terms of civil rights is surely more protected by the courts and by the laws today than it was then. Compared with fifty years ago, the opportunity for education today is more open and available for minority groups than it was then, largely through the efforts of government and the political process. However, belief that the prime goal of public education is to promote a sense of civic community and obligation for the public good has precipitously declined. The catchwords today are personalized learning, individualized instruction, and above all, alternatives. The decline in faith in public education is partly cause and partly result of the diminished sense of community in the nation as a whole. I believe the two are indelibly interrelated.

Whether the search for public education's role in achieving a civic community can be made compatible with the search for pluralistic communities is one of the major questions of the third century of the Republic. Much depends upon the realities of the political process undertaken in dozens of states and hundreds of school districts as well as in the Congress and the federal courts. But in the long run, it may depend even more upon the leadership of the profession in its relationships with the public.Here the contrast is remarkable. The child-centered school of the Progressive era is alive and well among educators, while parents clamor "back to the basics." Neither seems to pay much attention to the need for a new civism. The judgment of many observers, however, is that the lesson of Watergate is the need for the moral authority and leadership of a class of professionals imbued with a sense of civic community and justice.

In the midst of the Watergate crisis, Archibald Cox called upon the legal profession to educate the public with respect to the impeachment process:

> I am convinced that the legitimacy of the final conclusion in the view of the American people will depend upon the success of counsel and *other public men* in formulating general standards of conduct fairly applicable to any President, and in *educating the public upon their meaning and legal and moral base . . .*[31]

In this vein I believe that the legitimacy of public education and its moral authority can only be restored as the educational profession undertakes the continuing education of the public and of successive youthful generations in the values, commitments, and the actions necessary for the maintenance and improvement of a free and just political community. If there ever was a time for the most careful, serious, and pervasive kind of civic education devoted to the civil liberties and civil rights of Americans as well as to the universal human rights of the peoples of the world, it is *now* as we enter the third century of the Republic.

Is this view simply a nostalgia for the good old days of citizenship education? I believe not. It springs on the one hand from the deepest aspirations of many in the pluralistic minorities and on the other hand from the most sophisticated moral philosophy of the day. I note just two examples, one from politics and one from philosophy.

When a black woman was chosen in July 1976 to be the keynote

[31] *The New York Times,* January 24, 1974.

speaker at the Democratic National Convention, what was Barbara Jordan's message?

> A nation is formed by the willingness of each of us to share in the responsibility for upholding the common good . . . .
>
> Let there be no illusions about the difficulty of forming this national community. A spirit of harmony can only survive if each of us remembers, when bitterness and self-interest seem to prevail, that we share a common destiny.
>
> I have confidence that we can form a national community.[32]

And what philosophical rationale should undergird the common belief systems of educators, of government officials, and of the public itself? John Rawls, political and moral philosopher at Harvard, argues that it is a public sense of justice that produces a well-ordered society in which everyone accepts and knows that the others accept the same principles of justice. This means that the members of a well-ordered society must develop strong moral sentiments and normally effective desires to act as the principles of justice require.[33]

In response to the diversity of the pluralists' many communities, Rawls finds that it is only through a shared sense of justice that they can satisfactorily live together in political community:

> If men's inclination to self-interest makes their vigilance against one another necessary, their public sense of justice makes their secure association together possible. Among individuals with disparate aims and purposes a shared conception of justice establishes the bonds of civic friendship; the general desire for justice limits the pursuit of other ends. One may think of a public conception of justice as constituting the fundamental charter of a well-ordered human association.[34]

What the public sense of justice does is to establish the claims of what is *right* as prior to the claims of what is *good,* as defined by different individuals and different groups as they formulate their plans of life that promise to satisfy their particular rational desires. The principles of what is right and what is just thus put limits and impose restrictions on what are the reasonable conceptions of one's good as it may affect others. A just social system thus defines the

[32] *The New York Times,* July 15, 1976.

[33] John Rawls. *A Theory of Justice.* Cambridge, Massachusetts: Harvard University Press, 1971. p. 458.

[34] *Ibid.,* p. 5.

boundaries within which individuals and pluralistic communities must develop their aims and desires.

Rawls defines two principles of justice that set these boundaries, and it is to be noticed that the first principle is prior in importance to the second. The first principle must be satisfied before moving on to the second.

The first principle is the principle of equal liberties of citizenship. The second has to do with the regulation of social and economic advantages on behalf of equality.

The first principle is stated as follows:

> Each person is to have an equal right to the most extensive total system of equal basic liberties compatible with a similar system of liberty for all.[35]

What are the "equal liberties" of citizenship? They bear close resemblance to the American constitutional order based upon the Bill of Rights:

> The basic liberties of citizens are, roughly speaking, political liberty (the right to vote and to be eligible for public office) together with freedom of speech and assembly; liberty of conscience and freedom of thought; freedom of the person along with the right to hold (personal) property; and freedom from arbitrary arrest and seizure as defined by the concept of the rule of law. These liberties are all required to be equal by the first principle, since citizens of a just society are to have the same basic rights.[36]

After the citizen principle of equal political liberties is satisfied, then the second principle of justice should come into play:

> Social and economic *in*equalities are to be arranged so that they are both:
>
> 1. To the greatest benefit of the least advantaged . . . and
>
> 2. Attached to offices and positions open to all under conditions of fair equality of opportunity.[37]

Once the *political* principle of justice is satisfied, then a just society will move on to distribute income and wealth and satisfy a

[35] *Ibid.*, p. 302.

[36] *Ibid.*, p. 61.

[37] *Ibid.*, p. 302.

design of organization that makes use of differences in authority and responsibility:

> While the distribution of wealth and income need not be equal, it must be to everyone's advantage, and at the same time, positions of authority and offices of command must be accessible to all. One applies the second principle by holding positions open, and then, subject to this constraint, arranges social and economic inequalities so that everyone benefits.[38]

The total position elaborated in great detail by Rawls cannot even be hinted at here, and of course it has been powerfully criticized by some philosophers and social scientists.[39] But my point is that his position points unmistakably to the priority of the common civic community based upon the citizenship principle of justice as the prime authority for the purposes of public education in sharp contrast to the pluralistic views of a Novak, or a Nisbet, or an Itzkoff, a Cremin, or a Sizer. Rawls has not elaborated a full scale philosophy of education based upon his underlying political and moral philosophy as Dewey did. Nor perhaps has he linked thought and action sufficiently nor given as much role to intuition or affect as William Torbert charges. But I believe he has paved the way for the philosophers and practitioners of education to restore a profound civic, moral, and political basis to public education if we but will.

It is clear that there is affinity between Rawls and Kohlberg, and Kohlberg claims to be in the tradition of Dewey, but the search for a comprehensive role for public education in achieving civic community still lies before us. It might just be that recapturing a sense of legitimacy and of moral authority for public education may rest upon the success with which the educational profession can make effective at last what so many of the American people have hoped for it for 200 years—a priority in purpose for the vigorous promotion of the basic values of the American civic community—liberty *and* equality *and* justice. It may just be, too, that not only is the future of public education at stake, but the future of the democratic political community itself.

[38] *Ibid.*, p. 61.

[39] See, for example: Robert Nozick. *Anarchy, State and Utopia.* New York: Basic Books, 1974; and William R. Torbert. "Doing Rawls Justice." *Harvard Educational Review* 44 (4) ; November 1974.

Moral Education: The Role of the School

Donald H. Peckenpaugh

The Definition of a Moral Person

Recently, I've asked many people, "What is a moral person?" and have received a wide variety of answers. To my way of thinking, one little girl came up with the best answer when she said, "to love other people and to act so they can love you." When pushed for more ideas on the definition, she said, "You know, to know what's right and to do it."

I cannot give a better answer myself, and neither can most educators. When members of our educational fraternity were asked to choose a definition of the term "moral" last year, there was general agreement on: "Shows genuine concern about the rights and welfare of others" (97 percent); "Thinks clearly about issues of right and wrong" (89 percent); and "Obeys the dictates of his own conscience" (71 percent). I believe that the two sets of definitions are parallel; but, I believe that the professional definitions were not as good as the amateur. I'll go along with "to love other people and to act so they can love you," and "to know what's right and to do it."

Somewhere, that child of ten had already received the foundation of an excellent moral education. Most likely, it came from her family, her church, her school, and her playmates.

Educators rank the family and the church as having a powerful positive influence on the moral thinking and behavior of children; the school and the child's friends as having a less powerful but positive influence; and the mass media and government agencies as having a somewhat negative influence. When asked what order of influence they should have, the same order is repeated: the family, the church, the school, and the child's friends.

The School's Role in Moral Education

Does the school have a responsibility for moral education? Both as an individual and as an educator, my answer must be an unqualified "Yes." Moral education takes place all the time in the schools, even though it is not labeled as such. It is one aspect of the relationship between people; it is a part of the hidden curriculum. It is integrated into the organizational structure. It exists.

The process may have more impact than the content. The most important learnings that the schools foster are in the way they treat people, rather than what they say about behavior. The saying, "What you do speaks louder than what you say," has much truth here. Examples of this phenomenon are numerous. We often talk of the dignity of man, even while destroying it. We talk of the virtue of kindness and are sarcastic. We talk of honesty and truth and demonstrate in our daily lives that we subscribe to a different set of values. It slowly becomes obvious which values we hold. Children model after us, the real us, and the moral education that we really teach takes hold. They become "as we do, not as we say."

The public ranks moral instruction as one of the major goals of education. If one examines the major statements of the goals of education released over the years, moral or character education regularly appears.

The Phi Delta Kappa ranking of 18 goals of education shows three goals consistently rising to the top of the list. These are:

1. Develop skills in reading, writing, speaking, and listening.
2. Develop pride in work and a feeling of self-worth.
3. Develop moral responsibility and a sound ethical and moral behavior.

My experience in a variety of settings with different reference groups replicates this finding.

Which moral issues should be dealt with in the school? When presented with a dozen moral issues, educators were in agreement that almost all of the issues should be taught.

Ninety-eight to one hundred percent supported teaching about:

- Respect for Property
- Respect for Duly Constituted Authorities
- Lying and Cheating
- Physically Harming Another
- International Wrongdoing and Warfare
- Violating Someone's Civil Rights
- Taking Responsibility for One's Own Action.

Eighty-nine to ninety-six percent supported teaching about:

- Duty to Country
- Taking Responsibility for the Welfare of One's Fellow Human Being
- Duty to Family
- Sexual Mores and Behavior, and
- Distribution of the World's Wealth.

When asked about the overall view on the issues of the place of moral instruction in the schools, the most popular answer (by 88 percent of the respondents) was that "an active program of moral education in the schools is desirable as an assistance to the efforts of family and church, only then the school."

The Ways Schools Contribute to Moral Education

The school is in a unique position to supplement the home and the church in shaping the moral character of youth. It does so by teaching the cultural heritage of mankind. In that heritage are enshrined the values upon which our civilization is built. Because they are a part of the heritage, every individual shares them to some degree.

Besides teaching the values that are a part of our tradition and heritage, the school nurtures the critical thinking and judgment that are required in the weighing of values in every moral situation.

The school also has the advantage of being able to provide a testing ground for values, for it enables the child to test the practicality of ideals and standards to which the youngster has been exposed. Living, working, and playing with others may force the child to make realistic modifications of beliefs developed academically.

The school contributes to character education through the values of the teachers, the school, and society as a whole, as perceived by the child. In attempting to sort out and analyze values, the child is more likely to be influenced by what he or she sees than by what he or she is told. We know that character is caught as much as taught. It is caught by children from people who are important in their eyes and with whom they have an emotional bond. They imitate these people, usually unconsciously.

Throughout American education, a variety of approaches has been used for moral education. The methods first used stressed direct and explicit procedures. It was indoctrination, although its proponents would not describe it as that. Teachers wanted their students to internalize certain social, political, and moral imperatives, and so they lectured, appealed, and lauded the traditional virtues such as truth, responsibility, and love of country. This method is still being used.

Later, three types of major indirect techniques were used. For example, first, teachers demonstrated in their own behavior the norms that they wished to teach, such as orderliness, fairness, or humane treatment, and children identified with that adult role model. Second, the classroom environment provided a milieu that socialized students by forcing them to live the virtues such as obedience, orderliness, or delay of gratification, in order to succeed. Third, the choice of learning activities for students and the materials used transmitted effectively the values of the middle-class teachers.

During the past few years, several new approaches have been developed. These methods have surfaced with a variety of labels, including value clarification, analysis of controversial issues, humanistic education, and development of the positive self-concept.

What Morality Gets Taught in This Indirect Way?

Usually it is the middle-class morality that is taught in the American public school. The content of the moral conscience of the middle class varies from place to place and from time to time. There is general agreement, however, as to what is "right" and "wrong," "good" or "bad," and it has been this middle-class creed that has been transmitted from generation to generation. It is not written anywhere but in our hearts, yet we know it as our parents and teachers taught it to us. "Work faithfully, waste nothing, and make the best of your opportunities; study and make ready, and some day your chance will come; be neat, be clean, and respect authority; don't make waves; don't lie, cheat, or steal; respect your parents; don't hit anybody smaller than you; and love God and your country." Where does this set of values come from? Some of it comes from the spirit of capitalism, some from the Protestant ethic, some from our American heritage. All of it comes from our parents and other significant adults, and from our peer relationships.

Teachers add on an even more specific litany of their own: "Be quiet; be orderly; always do your best; do your homework; don't run in the halls; don't fight unless he hit you first; don't 'goof around' in the bathroom; don't play rough with the girls; and skip a line after your name before you begin to write."

Should these be the values transmitted in our schools? This has been one of the most difficult problems in urban education, and one of the real concerns of educating the culturally distinct. Each of us defines what is "good" or "right" by the values we hold. Teachers and school administrators have come primarily from the lower middle class. We transmit our values because we know they are right. The middle class teacher is a tremendous force when unleashed. Pity the lower class child, the minority student, and the child from the "new generation" when the teacher forces his or her values upon them.

Kohlberg

Is there a better way for the schools to contribute to moral education? Besides these indirect ways of contributing to the moral education of youth, a number of better approaches have been developed. They are better because they are direct, conscious, and systematic.

Lawrence Kohlberg, a professor at Harvard University, has laid a foundation for much of the best thought in the field of moral education. Kohlberg and his colleagues have studied ethical awareness by longitudinal studies in the United States, Great Britain, Canada, Taiwan, Mexico, and Turkey. From this work they postulated a hierarchy of six stages through which a person must pass in the development of ethical awareness.

At stage one, good and bad are defined in terms of avoiding of punishment and deference to power. At stage two, right consists of that which satisfies one's own needs and occasionally the needs of others. At stage three, good behavior is that which pleases others and is approved by them. At stage four, right behavior consists of doing one's duty and maintaining the social order. At stage five, right action tends to be defined in terms of general rights and standards that have been critically examined and agreed upon by the whole society. It is at level six that right is defined by the decision of conscience in accord with self-chosen ethical principles, appealing to logical comprehensiveness.

The motive given for rule obedience or moral action at each stage is as follows:

1. Obey rules to avoid punishment.
2. Conform to obtain rewards, have favors returned, and so on.
3. Conform to avoid disapproval, dislike by others.
4. Conform to avoid censure by legitimate authorities and resultant guilt.
5. Conform to maintain the respect of the impartial spectator judging in terms of community welfare.
6. Conform to avoid self-condemnation.

To summarize, at the preconventional level, stages one and two, the child is responsive to cultural rules and labels of good and bad, right or wrong, but interprets these labels either in terms of the physical or the hedonistic consequences of action (punishment, reward, exchange of favors) or in terms of the physical power of those who enunciate the rules and labels. At the conventional level, stages three and four, maintaining the expectations of the individual's family, group, or nation is perceived as valuable in its own right, regardless of immediate and obvious consequences. The attitude is not only one of conformity to personal expectations and social order, but of loyalty to it, of actively maintaining, supporting, and justifying the order, and of identifying with the persons or groups involved in it. At the postconventional, autonomous, or principled level, stages five and six, there is a clear effort to define moral values and principles that have validity and application apart from the authority of the groups or persons holding these principles and apart from the individual's own identification with these groups.

Kohlberg's theories are now being introduced into a variety of U.S. classrooms. Many teachers have been stimulated by the concept and have developed their own classroom programs using Kohlberg's moral stages. A set of filmstrips published by Guidance Associates has provided needed assistance. The Unitarian churches in Birmingham, Michigan, and in Grosse Pointe, Michigan, have developed youth education programs based on these developmental stages.

Edwin Fenton, from Harvard's Center for Moral Development and Education, applies Kohlberg's concept of moral development with young adolescents through moral discussions. Although he has actively worked with some young people, his major contribution is in stimulating thought of others about the application.

Fenton proposes two ways that schools can help the natural process of moral development. The first is to conduct moral discussions that allow young people to think about various issues as a part of their social studies and English classes. For example, he sees literature as loaded with moral dilemmas. A teacher with the skill to conduct a useful discussion can assist pupils in achieving a higher level of cognitive moral development.

A second approach to moral education suggested by Fenton is the "civic education" school, an application of Kohlberg's "just community school" concept. This is an alternative school within a regular school, designed so that students can think about their rights, and even more important, to think about their responsibilities.

Cambridge High and Latin School, Cambridge, Massachusetts

A new alternative school within Cambridge High and Latin School called the "Cluster School," was formed to "implement Kohlberg's concept of a "Just Community School." This approach integrates social studies and English curricula with a program of moral discussions and a governance structure based on a participatory democracy."

In the "Cluster School," all students participate in the core curriculum in English and social studies. This core curriculum centers on moral discussions, on role-taking and communication, and on relating the governance structure of the school to that of the wider society.

The conventional administrative pyramid has been replaced by a flexible structure that encourages the sharing of authority, power, and responsibility. The administrative structure of the Cluster School complements the school's democratic structure. Each month, the staff selects a new person to represent the school in all meetings within the school system that require the presence of an "administrator." No major decisions or commitments are made without consulting the entire community.

The Cluster School "revolves around community meetings, small group meetings, advisor groups, the discipline committee, and the staff-student-consultant meetings." The school has its own rules, which are made by staff and student vote.

The staff has observed positive changes in the behavior of students who had long histories of difficulty in school. These students say that the changes in their behavior came about mainly because the Cluster School treats them fairly and gives them a forum in which they can protest unfair treatment. The staff has reported that many students in the school have begun to progress in moral reasoning up the Kohlberg scale, but research to test this hypothesis has just begun.

Brookline High School, Brookline, Massachusetts

The Brookline Moral Education Project is a three-year program funded by the Danforth Foundation as a demonstration of teacher training and curriculum writing in moral education. The project began with moral development seminars for 30 Brookline High teachers and administrators. Objectives were to review psychological research on moral development, examine curriculum materials, and create new ones, particularly moral dilemmas, for American history, world history, law, guidance, psychology, and independent study. Moral education was perceived as an integral part of social studies and guidance rather than an add-on to the curriculum.

A new moral curriculum for Brookline's five-year-old alternative school involved a close affiliation between Brookline and the

Cambridge Cluster School at Cambridge High and Latin School, initially funded by the Kennedy Foundation as an experiment in "the just school." Additional Danforth funding made it possible for the Cluster School staff to work up a core curriculum in law, based on the work of Charles Quigley of the Law in a Free Society Project of the State Bar of California.

Values Clarification

The second major force in the field of moral education is found in values clarification. For the past seven years or so, one of the most popular new programs on the American educational scene has been values clarification. Sidney Simon, Merrill Harmin, Louis Raths, and others have encouraged teachers to depart drastically from the traditional approach of giving answers, of moralizing, and of criticizing. Instead, their innovative approach seeks to create an environment in which the student is helped to understand his or her own value preferences. Through a variety of value-free procedures, teachers have learned to assist pupils in identifying their own preferred values and those of others.

Simon has repeatedly insisted that values clarification means designing a curriculum around youngsters' minds. It means faith in the process of inquiry, creating a climate that allows students to ask about things they feel. It means giving them a chance to learn about their own personal, individual values. It means helping children choose their own values instead of imposing preconceived values upon them. Simon, professor at the Center for Humanistic Education at the University of Massachusetts, states emphatically that values clarification also means that adults must be honest with themselves about their own values, because children see easily through a paradoxical society where the gap between what we say and what we do is big enough to decay in.

Values clarification is an especially effective approach in an era of changing values. Learning values is quite different from learning the capitals of the states or the multiplication table. Values are not so much learned as they are internalized through the intimate and complex process of identification. A child strives to integrate and stabilize his own self-image by becoming "as one" with other persons —parents, older siblings, friends, and teachers. The process is carried on, for the most part unconsciously, on the level of feeling and emotion, and seldom intellectualized. Because of the process involved, the values held and demonstrated by the significant adults in a child's life are crucial.

The most significant contribution of the values clarification movement may be in helping teachers make instruction more relevant. The movement attempts to do this by encouraging teachers to change the instructional focus from facts and concepts to the values level. Students are encouraged to examine their personal values and their present life in relationship to the subject matter being studied.

In general, the purposes of values clarification are: (a) to sensitize people to value issues; (b) to give them experience in thinking critically about such issues; (c) to give them opportunities to share perceptions with others and learn cooperative problem-solving skills; and (d) to help them learn to apply the valuing processes in their own lives. The teaching process in values clarification involves helping students to *confront* a moral problem, to *state* a position, to *test* the reasoning behind their position, and to *reflect* on their reasoning and that of others during a discussion.

Advocates praise the approach for being appropriate for the American youth of today in a youth culture that emphasizes freedom, equality, and autonomy. It is also praised because it has been accepted by pupils and teachers, while the older methods have not seemed to be effective. The examination of values is done through a series of often imaginative and creative techniques Simon calls values-clarification strategies. Many of these can be found in two of his books that focus on strategies: *Values Clarification: A Handbook* and *Meeting Yourself Halfway.*

Ossining High School, Ossining, New York

The staff members of Ossining have created a model program to assist students in clarifying values. Initially, representative clergy, community leaders, students, and teachers were invited to develop a commitment to values education to be implemented by values clarification. Teachers volunteered to participate in a summer workshop and develop a report of sample lessons in the various disciplines. Two courses are now being offered that emphasize values clarification—"You and the Law," and a revised ninth-grade basic social studies course, "Asian Studies."

The objectives of "You and the Law," an elective course, are to identify simple, everyday legal issues; translate basic issues into a student's own terms; analyze new conflict situations; construct hypotheses, test conclusions, and synthesize principles into sound and useful generalizations on law in society; recognize an awareness of values conflict in simple legal problems of institutions; write or speak a preference for identified values; and compare the student's own values to those of a democratic society.

The purpose of "Asian Studies," a required course for all freshmen, is to enable students to understand the importance of culture, the values of the people in the culture, and the effects of environment and time on the values of the people and their culture.

Neenah Senior High School, Armstrong Campus, Neenah, Wisconsin

This two-year, senior high school is implementing the "just school" approach. It employs values clarification strategies with the involvement of students, staff, and parents in the development of basic rules for governing school behavior. A Personal Responsibility Committee of the Student-Faculty-Administration Council delineated ways in which school causes students to be less than responsible, established an "I Care" project (in which 70 percent of the students signed a pledge to be responsible members of the school community). The council developed homeroom projects in community affairs and organized a Political Awareness Forum. Boundary Breaking, a leadership program for students who would not otherwise be brought together during the school day, is an important part of the "just school" implementation.

Wagner High School, Wurtsmith Memorial Schools, (Department of the Air Force, DOD Dependents' Schools-Pacific Area)

The Wagner High School staff has developed elective courses using moral dilemmas and the values clarification techniques to instill in students a respect for the moral and legal values of the culture and a desire for learning now and in the future: "An Introduction to the Behavioral Sciences: Anthropology, Psychology, and Sociology"; "The Future of Man"; "Futurology"; "Values in U.S. Society"; and "Human Relations."

Unami Junior High School, Chalfont, Pennsylvania

"Humanities" is a required course for seventh and ninth graders who meet for three forty-five-minute periods a week. It emphasizes the values clarification approach to self-awareness and personal decision-making. Classroom sessions are supplemented by guest speakers, films, field trips, and an occupational experience day. No tests are given, and it is conducted on a pass-fail basis. A values clarification and group dynamics approach is used. Although called "Humanities," topics of current concern such as venereal disease, corporal punishment, and career choice are considered.

Lakewood City Public Schools, Lakewood, Ohio

The Lakewood Public Schools and the Educational Research Council of America have developed an affective curriculum designed to meet the problems of youthful frustration and aggression. Funded by the Ohio Department of Education through an ESEA Title III Project, "Curriculum for Meeting Modern Problems" is a series on three educational levels: "Dealing with Causes of Behavior" for grades 1-5; "Dealing with Aggressive Behavior" for middle and junior high schools; and "The New Model Me" for senior high schools. "The New Model Me," which consists of units on behavior, controls, the real self, values, responses, and change, can be taught as separate course or integrated easily into any subject area. The Lakewood staff created the curriculum using the causal approach to human behavior, pioneered by the late Ralph Ojemann. Values clarification, democratic problem solving, and decision making are the principal techniques utilized. "The New Model Me" is one of the 21 original Developer/Demonstrator Projects in the United States Office of Education's National Diffusion Network.

Values clarification has been criticized because it often leaves the student in conflict about matters of deep concern to him or her. The "bootstrap" process does not work if there has not been sufficient input, earlier, from some source. Values do not simply exist in an individual; they must be originally learned. I have found the values clarification approach of most value with older students who have already established a base. Recognizing the nature of learning, one must have absorbed a values position before it can be clarified.

These teaching techniques also have been criticized because they are techniques—that is, that they are merely a gimmick or device, skimming the surface in a superficial manner. I have found in my work with high school pupils in values clarification that preferences, although legitimate expressions of belief, are frequently confused, inconsistent, and usually unclear.

Other Approaches

Lifeline—A well thought-out, graded curriculum for secondary students has been developed by Peter McPhail of the Schools Council Moral Education project at Cambridge University and now marketed by Argus Communications in this country as "Startline," a program for 8- to 13-year olds. Mr. McPhail and his associates have taken an empirical approach to moral education using values. They surveyed 1,600 adolescents in England and Wales to discover what "value" problems concern young people. They investigated to determine the most effective way in which value issues can be approached. Lifeline employs everyday social learning situations to help motivate adolescents to behave with consideration. A series of case studies has been developed that are designed to initiate student discussion. These cases focus on the issues raised in the student surveys. The material is utilized in numerous curricular areas, where appropriate.

The theory, which was developed from significant situation social psychological research undertaken in Oxford University with Michael Argyle, is outlined in *Learning to Care.* It is a theory of adolescent moral learning process, and is not based on traditional ethical argument or verbal analysis alone. It uses as its basis the adolescent consensus that good (moral) treatment was "treatment that took an individual's needs, feelings, and interests into consideration." McPhail feels that this fits in very well with the traditional Christian moral position and also stresses the practical interpretation of Kant's categorical imperative. With this emphasis on learning behavior rather than moral theory, this approach represents a different area of development from that of the English verbal analytic school of Kohlberg's stages theory.

Character Education Curriculum—The American Institute for Character Education of San Antonio, Texas, a nonprofit educational foundation, has developed an elementary school program that promotes cooperation between the school and the home, the Character Education Curriculum. It is composed of lessons for use in the classroom. The program promotes the values of twelve standards of character and conduct in their code: honesty, generosity, justice, honor, kindness, firm belief in the right, courage, tolerance, use of time and talents, rights and duties of citizens, obligations of citizens of a free country, and standing for truth. Sophisticated instructional approaches such as role-playing, case study discussion, story completion, art projects, and multi-media presentations are effectively incorporated.

The program has been complimented for the quality of the developmental efforts, but some critics have felt that some of the material is too simple for the young age group at which it is directed. A more substantial criticism is whether the approach itself works. The evidence seems to indicate that it does. First, teachers who have used the materials rate them highly. Second, over half of the teachers reported that student attitudes have improved and also reported less vandalism, cheating, and stealing.

A careful reading of the teacher's text seems to indicate that the children themselves are led to discover the desirability of good behavior and to make sound moral judgments. This should lead them to the establishment of right attitudes and good behavior, most important for younger children of the elementary grades.

St. Louis Park High School, St. Louis Park, Minnesota—"Religion in Human Culture" is a high school level, social studies course about world religions that has been developed and field tested by the World Religions' Curriculum Development Center. The Center, sponsored by St. Louis Park Public Schools, has been supported by ESEA, Title IV C, and the Northwest Area Foundation. The general course goals seek the enhancement of human dignity, the utilization of rational processes in learning activities, and to maintain the imprecise, delicate, and human qualities that religions represent. The course is designed to help students learn about the religious diversity of the world, develop attitudes of respect and understanding of beliefs and practices of themselves and others, and realize the legitimacy of those beliefs. The ultimate goal is that students develop attitudes and action patterns that will improve human relationships.

Development of the course involved student and community advisory committees, parents, and consultants from the study of religion, the social sciences, and history. Evaluation was conducted by an independent contractor. The evaluation program in field test schools in Minnesota and seven other states shows statistically significant changes among students in both cognitive and affective areas.

Based on three successive rounds of field testing, the materials have been completely revised. They will be published and commercially available from Argus Communications in late 1977. The package of materials can be purchased in total or in parts, and will include paperback booklets or readings, teacher guides, sound synchronized filmstrips, and duplicating masters. The units included in the initial package include an introductory unit of religious expression, Hinduism, Buddism, Judaism, Christianity, Islam, and independent study.

Bible Stories as Case Studies—The Church of Jesus Christ of Latter-Day Saints, the Mormons, uses Bible stories for teaching. This training program uses stories and case studies to complete the faith, as well as the character of youngsters. The stories provide the basis for open discussion, with the intention of helping the young people to become better members of their families, their country, and their church. The approach is consistent with the view that most people have a desire to improve if they have an example of something better.

"Le Havdil"—The Jewish program "Le Havdil: To Make a Difference" is a beautiful blend of the old and the new, developed by the Rocky Mountain Curriculum Planning Workshop in 1972. Its educational approach is completely modern although much of the content is the ancient and traditional Jewish cultural heritage. The instruction is oriented toward "freedom of choice." It includes encounter groups, role playing, and games as techniques. The publishers state that "this material on Jewish ethics is an attempt to incorporate the Jewish tradition into a meaningful package so that students may choose their individual ethical systems with a firm understanding of the option which exists in the Jewish tradition."

"Le Havdil" is rapidly gaining acceptance, in part for its modern teaching techniques, and also because of its dependence upon older sources, traditionally accepted.

"Moral Education Project of the Ontario Institute for Studies in Education"—The work done in moral education at the Ontario Institute for Studies in Education in Toronto should be examined closely by any educator planning the introduction of moral or values programs into the schools. Not only do they provide a set of approaches that are worth considering, they raise questions for practitioners that should be of concern.

The project developed out of the work of Clive Beck, initiated while he was conducting a high school course in ethics in 1969-70. Later, the project was expanded to include classes at both high school and elementary levels. In recent years, a considerable amount of research has been done on preservice and inservice teacher education.

In a very practical booklet, *Moral Education in the Schools,* Beck suggests sets of topics for five age levels of pupils from ages 5 to 18. Personal and social values in general are presented for ages five to nine with topics such as "Helping Other People," and "The Values of Rules to Ourselves and Others." Human relations, concentrating on social aspects of values with topics such as "The Individual's Need for Other People," and "The Place of Governments and Other Authority" provide the basis for ages 10 and 11. For ages 12 and 13, the topics are in decision-making, concentrating on personal aspects of values with the emphasis on such items as "Worthwhile Personal Goals to Pursue in Life," and "Emotional Elements in One's Makeup." For ages 14 and 15, the topic is human issues in the world today and again is social in emphasis, but this segment employs examples with wider, often global, application. Typical content would be "Freedom and Equality in the World Today," and "Means to Ends: Political Process." Finally, value theory is again presented in the fifth stage, which is designed for students ages 16 to 18. This set of topics represents a return to a more general consideration of the nature of values, the criteria of good and bad, right and wrong, and one's approach to value questions. It is like the first segment, but is at a much higher level of sophistication. Topics include such concepts as "The Purpose of Morality," and "Justice."

A key notion of their work is "structure." They attempt to give students an initial sense of order through what they call a "principled discussion method." They outline topics for discussions, offering guiding questions, and give study notes on each topic to provide a sense of direction. A contextual rather than an individualistic approach is used; that is, although they call theirs a values approach, they follow the work of Lawrence Kohlberg rather than Sidney Simon. Their methods focus upon cognitive aspects of moral development, rather than guidance or sensitivity training. Departing from Kohlberg, they do not confine themselves to a single moral dilemma approach, but experiment with a variety of methods designed to stimulate analysis, discussion, and response to moral values.

Evaluation of the project results has been done on both a formal and informal basis. Pretests and posttests of experimental and control groups showed significant growth of pupils when tested on Kohlberg's dilemmas. They do see their work as tentative and exploratory, and not definitive.

Beck and Sullivan raise several crucial questions. First, the predominance of teachers remains at the conventional stages of morality (3 and 4). Their emphasis on the "law and order" level may inhibit some aspects of the educational process. Such teachers may be unable to stimulate growth and may at times even hinder pupil development. Also, Beck and Sullivan raise the question of how the evaluation of levels of moral development is perceived by teachers. If they negatively evaluate one stage as of less value than another in a stereotype rather than taking a developmental perspective, a gross misjustice may be done to the child. They stress the danger of stereotyping inherent in any stage theory, and in recent years have been inclined to abandon the Kohlberg position entirely.

Examples from Abroad

Examples from abroad also are helpful. One of the major agents of moral education in modern societies is the school. This is obvious in the modern democracies, especially England. Likewise, it is true in the two largest communist countries, China and Russia. In all three, the impact of the peer group is substantial.

In England, ethics has been taught for generations through a system of expectations for behavior regulated by the students themselves. With guidance from the adults, older students administer the system, including giving corporal punishment. Although the adult's authority remains the base, the peer group itself exerts pressure on the individual for proper behavior. Most of the schools run by the government in England have had a substantial religious education program, including ethics and morality. The independent schools, particularly those with church ties, frequently made religious and moral values one of their basic programs.

In both China and Russia, the schools carry a large responsibility for moral education. In both these communist countries, there is heavy emphasis on teaching the communist morality, with special stress on national economic production, and loyalty to the country and the party. Equally strong is the emphasis upon individual ethical responsibilities and family loyalty.

Although little is known about the details of Russian education, it is obvious that group ethics is promoted over that of the individual. For example, the class and the section are held responsible for the individual member's conduct. Therefore, the group is punished for the misbehavior of an individual. Moral and ethical behavior are parts of the daily learning activities, and teachers are held responsible to incorporate this instruction as a part of the total learning experiences of the school.

In Russia, the principal agent of character development has been the peer group rather than the family. Soviet society fosters ideologically approved goals, through the group in a constructive manner.

Even less is known of moral education in China. However, it is known that there is a substantial program of indoctrination—readings, memorization, lectures, and discussions that propagandize for communism, for the Peoples Republic, and for Chairman Mao. Also, the virtues of duty, altruism, and honesty are inculcated. Family loyalty is taught as well as the collectivist loyalty.

In both China and Russia, there is heavy emphasis on moral education, both formal and informal. Three techniques are emphasized in instruction: exhortation, example, and experience. Quotations, slogans, and posters are given great prominence. Children are saturated with moral advice, just as the general population is exhorted. Exemplary behavior in modern heroes, in historical figures, or even literary characters is cited for inspiration. Practical experience is used in a variety of ways. The virtues and habits of good behavior are taught with emphasis on collective consciousness from the early games and songs for preschool-aged children to the combined work and study program of older students. Youth organizations and children's centers have a special role in both moral and political education.

Conclusion

As a lifelong educator, I feel about as confident in giving advice as I do as an experienced father. In the early stages of my first child's life, I gave a talk entitled, "The Ten Commandments of Rearing Children." With the birth of my second daughter, the talk became "Suggestions on Living with Your Child." Today, twenty years later, I am silent on the subject.

But confident or not, if we draw together the strands that run through most of these approaches, we can safely conclude that a quality program of moral education will have certain characteristics.

- It will be an active program that is of real assistance to the efforts of family and church.
- It will be rich in self-discovery, putting children in contact with their deepest values.
- Following the approach of self-discovery, we will not interfere with the parents' role or the church's role as moral educators.
- It will recognize and respect a variety of values.
- It will be integrated into the entire program. In social studies, for instance, we can approach the landing of the Pilgrims on three levels: as a fact—it happened in 1621; as a concept—it was an experience they shared with many other peoples fleeing religious persecution; and as a value—we can ask our students to search their own hearts and ask: what would be important enough to you that would cause you to leave your home, relatives, and friends behind, and go far away to start a new life?
- It will recognize the known stages of moral development in the life of the child.
- Finally, it will be a program of substantial content, including a study about religious and great philosophical systems, including moral thinkers of the past and present—and this for two reasons:

(a) As schools we have to hand on our children's cultural heritage; and (b) Morality requires much more than attitudes and feelings, it is the ability to judiciously and critically weigh conflicting values in difficult moral situations.

I would like to conclude with a minimosaic of three quotations that capture the spirit of what I have said:

"The most significant fact in this world today is, that in nearly every village under the American flag, the school house is larger than the church."—*Ingersoll*

"I desire to see the time when education, and by its means, morality, sobriety, enterprise, and industry, shall become much more general than at present."—*Abraham Lincoln*

"I only took the regular course," said the mock turtle. "What was that," inquired Alice. "Reeling and Writhing, of course, to begin with, and then the different branches of Arithmetic—Ambition, Distraction, Uglification, and Derision."—*Lewis Carroll*

Values Education: 1976 and Beyond

Howard Kirschenbaum

The aim of this paper is to outline the state of the art in values education and to make recommendations for further research, development, and dissemination activities in this area.

The first challenge is to delineate the field known as "values education." I think of this as a rather broad area, including some aspects of affective education, the moral-development approach, the cognitive-decision-making approach, and the other approaches to moral and citizenship education.

Common Goals

At first glance, it might seem that one of the most difficult problems in the field of values education would be to get the theorists and practitioners from different schools to agree on a set of overriding goals. On the contrary, I would like to suggest that most values/moral/citizenship educators do share a common set of objectives, which can be clustered around two overall goals: (a) to help people become more fulfilled and satisfied with the quality of their lives, and (b) to help people become more constructive members of the groups

* This paper was originally presented at the National Conference on Moral and Citizenship Education, sponsored by Research for Better Schools, Philadelphia, Pennsylvania, under a grant from the National Institute of Education. For a list of materials available on values education, write Howard Kirschenbaum, National Humanistic Education Center, 110 Spring Street, Saratoga Springs, New York 12866

of which they are a part, that is, in their relationships, families, task groups, social groups, and societies.

These two general goals can be stated more explicitly. To expand the first goal, when life has value for us, we prize and cherish more of our choices, beliefs, and activities. We experience a stronger self-concept and feel greater meaning in our life. We are less apathetic and flighty, more purposeful and committed. This does not mean we are always "happy." It means that we are living vitally, experiencing the richness of ourselves, others, and the world around us as we move toward self-selected, meaningful goals. I suggest this is one generally agreed-upon goal of values education.

The second goal deals with being socially constructive, which, in my opinion, means to act in a way that promotes the values of life and liberty. Liberty would encompass the values of freedom, justice, and equality. Stated differently, to be socially constructive helps create the conditions that permit others the freedom to pursue lives that will be fulfilling and satisfying to *themselves,* provided they do not infringe on the rights of others.

I have never encountered a serious advocate of moral, citizenship, or values education who disagreed fundamentally with these two goals. It is true that some approaches have emphasized the development of personally satisfying values, while others have stressed the development of socially constructive attitudes and action. Still others have focused on both areas. However, no educational approach, to my knowledge, has stated as its goal the cultivation of unfulfilled, purposeless individuals or social misfits.

To cite an example, values clarification (Raths, Harmin, and Simon, 1966), one of the most popular values education approaches in the schools, has emphasized the importance of helping people discover and build into their lives that which they truly prize and cherish. This is clearly consistent with the first goal mentioned earlier. Values clarification is also explicit about encouraging people to consider the consequences of their choices—both personal and social consequences. Here both goals are addressed. In its methodology, values clarification encourages respect for all viewpoints and autonomy for individuals; it thereby implicitly affirms the importance of individual growth, but not at the expense of those around one. Explicitly and implicitly, this values education approach supports the two broad goals mentioned earlier.

Milton Rokeach (1975), a pioneer in the fields of attitude change and values theory, also reflects both goals of values education. He writes, "The school has not only always been in the business of inculcating, shaping, and modifying certain values, but *should* be in this business. Society depends upon the educational institution to successfully inculcate educational values" (p. 124). Among educational values he includes, "a sense of accomplishment, self-respect, wisdom, freedom, and equality" and refers to "what are perhaps the ultimate educational values—individual growth and self-realization" (p. 125).

Another values education approach popularized by Rucker, Arnspiger, and Brodbeck (1969), based on a theory of values developed by Harold Laswell (1951), affirms the importance of eight values as a goal for human development and education: respect, wealth, power, enlightenment, skill, rectitude, well-being, and affection. As Laswell defines these values, they fall very nicely in line with either or both of the goals for values education—personal effectiveness or social commitment.

Many religious education programs have similar goals for the values development of their constituents—young and old alike. The "good life" might be defined by most religions as acting charitably toward one's neighbor (the "Social Gospel"); pursuing a larger, transcendental purpose or meaning in life; and enjoying the goodness of all creation in the process (personal fulfillment). The YMCA, for example, has recently launched a major values education program of national scope, based largely on the values-clarification approach and affirming the importance of individual growth and social responsibility. Many new publications in religious education make the same connection (for example, Larson and Larson, 1976).

Relationship to Other Approaches

This agreement on the broader goals of values education is not confined only to those theorists who are typically identified as "values theorists." They are also shared by other moral/citizenship education schools of thought. Certainly the chief concern of the moral developmentalists has been the promotion of higher levels of moral reasoning—for example, the values of reciprocity, fairness, and the "just community." In an excellent yearbook (Metcalf, 1971) that describes a "values analysis" approach to values education, the president of the National Council for the Social Studies voices the same concerns: "Societies today, as they have for thousands of years, embrace a system of values that rejects killing, stealing, lying, and cheating. But men everywhere keep on killing, stealing, lying, and cheating. . . . While we invest a million dollars on cancer research presumably to preserve human life, we spend billions on systems designed to destroy life. . . . The same community that is aroused over the spread of venereal disease among its young will not allow sex education in its school curriculum" (pp. v-vi). His frustration with an education that has failed to achieve its potential in human welfare is apparent in every example, and he expresses the dissatisfaction of many values educators. They, too, are not happy with the status quo.

The Problems Addressed by Values Education

This dissatisfaction with the status quo is another thing most values educators have in common, although they express it in different ways.

People are confused and conflicted about their values, say the values clarifiers. In individual lives the symptoms are apathy, flightiness, over-conforming, over-dissenting, and other behaviors indicative of lack of values or values confusion. Ultimately, such confusion can lead to a lack of perceived purpose in living—a state of confusion, anguish, or suffering. Individual values problems also affect relationships and can contribute to considerable conflict within families and groups. Individual values problems can lead to inefficiency and a reduction of constructive activity in society. Society can ill afford such a loss. Nations across the globe suffer from similar values confusion—performing great acts of charity and construction with one hand, and moral atrocities and environmental destruction with the other. The very survival of the planet is endangered by such values conflict. So say the values clarifiers (for example, Kirschenbaum, Harmin, Howe, and Simon, 1975).

Other values educators agree. Rucker *et al.* (1969) see young people suffering from "value deprivations"—alienation, lack of self-respect, powerlessness—in other words, the opposite of Laswell's eight values mentioned above. Rokeach finds inconsistencies between the end-values people say they hold and the means they use to achieve these values. Moral developmentalists see most people operating at relatively low levels of moral reasoning. In an often-repeated study—which may be apocryphal but wouldn't surprise me if it were true—it was established that if the Bill of Rights were put to a referendum today, it would be defeated by a whopping majority. Not surprisingly, cognitive-decision-making theorists are concerned about the lack of logic and critical thinking being applied to social discourse and decision-making.

Values-Education Approaches

In short, values educators believe that conscious pedagogical strategies must be employed if we are to move from the present rather unhappy state of affairs to one characterized by the two broad goals of values education. In effect we have this dilemma: As children, as adults, and as a society, here we are frequently at Point A—lacking values clarity, lacking critical-thinking skills, operating at low levels of moral reasoning, with social issues and crises receiving only the most token recognition, thoughtful analysis, and corrective action. Our goal, on the other hand (on the other shore might be a better metaphor), is Point C—individuals with clearer purposes, enthusiasm, sharpness of thinking, higher levels of moral reasoning, and the social commitment to recognize problems, thoughtfully analyze them, and take bold and effective action. The problem of values education, therefore, is very simple: How do we help people move away from Point A and toward Point C? In the context of public education, how do we help students move along the developmental continuum to greater values maturity?

"B" is the intervention that the educator employs to move from Point A to Point C. Parents, teachers, religious leaders, and other helpers have been intervening for thousands of years, of course, attempting to influence the values development of their charges. More recently, psychologists and educators have developed interventions based on more precise theories of how values develop and change, theories usually tested by varying degrees of empirical research.

One of the most traditional approaches to values education, not one built on a strong foundation of theory and research but nevertheless one that worked successfully for centuries when the world was less complex and there were fewer choices to be made, is that of *moralizing*. Gently or forcefully, subtly or harshly, the moralizer tells young people what to do, what to think, and what is right or wrong, good or bad. There is often a great deal of wisdom or caring attached to such moralizing. The problem is that different teachers are telling children different things. And their parents, ministers, peer groups, the mass media, movie stars, sports heroes, politicians, and advertisements are also telling them different things—in fact, they are being bombarded from all sides with different messages about what values to pursue and what goals to strive for to be successful, to belong, to be popular, and to succeed with the other sex. The moralizer adds his or her individual input; but, then, how does the young person sort it all out?

Many do not. They grow into adults who are easily influenced by the most persuasive moralizers and therefore are filled with contradictions among their values and inconsistencies between their beliefs and behavior (which is a reflection of the many different moralizers they have been exposed to). They are easy prey to the ad man's version of reality, the demagogue's lie, or the peer group's pressure toward conformity.

Another traditional values education approach is that of *modeling*, in which the model is a living example of the values he or she believes. One of the best ways to teach anything is to present a concrete example of it. Young people today are quick to spot adults who say one thing, and do another. Unfortunately, though, the problem remains. There are too many models modeling different values—different goals, life styles, speech patterns, moral codes, and orientations toward work and play, life and death. Which models are the real teachers, and which are the charlatans? How does the young person decide?

Because the traditional approaches of moralizing and modeling fail to teach young people a process by which they can analyze much of the confusing information about their world and learn to make their own decisions—a process by which they can pick the best and reject the worst of all the moralizing and modeling they are continually subjected to—most of the values education approaches developed in recent years have provided a different type of intervention aimed at getting from Point A to Point C. They recognize that moralizing and modeling will continue to exist as alternative values education approaches, but argue that they are not sufficient to do the job. Let me describe some of these approaches in terms of how they go about their task.

Values clarification tries to teach people a *process* that can be applied to values choices throughout their lives. This process consists of seven subprocesses, first defined by Raths *et al.* (1966). These are (a) choosing from alternatives, (b) choosing after considering consequences, (c) choosing freely, (d) prizing and cherishing one's choices, (e) publicly affirming one's choices, (f) acting on one's choices, and (g) acting with a repetition and pattern in one's choices. The values-clarification methodology consists of hundreds of different classroom or group "strategies" or activities that are designed to help people learn these processes, and to give them practice applying them to values-laden areas in their lives (Simon, Howe, and Kirschenbaum, 1972). Values-clarification approaches for dealing with school subjects are also employed (Harmin, Kirschenbaum, and Simon, 1973). Research on values-clarification provides tentative support that this intervention helps achieve the goals of values education without any loss (and often with a gain) to school subject-matter goals (Kirschenbaum, 1977).

Milton Rokeach's work on values is not so much an educational approach at this stage as an experimental approach to investigate how values may be changed by outside manipulation. He continues to demonstrate that by showing individuals discrepancies between what they say they personally value and what other groups they identify with say *they* value, the individual's values will change in a predictable direction. In all of Rokeach's experiments, the change is in the direction of more socially constructive values and behavior, as defined earlier. (He refuses to conduct his experiments in the opposite direction, to see if the same discrepancy theory would still apply.)

Rucker *et al.* (1969) use many activities akin to values-clarification and many materials they and their colleagues have developed, all centered around Laswell's eight value dimensions. Students, thereby, continue to understand and internalize these eight values more deeply and see how the eight value dimensions are related to their own lives.

Moral developmentalists in the Kohlbergian tradition intervene by posing value dilemmas for students to consider and facilitating discussions in which several different levels of moral reasoning are likely to be present. Their research indicates that under the right conditions, progression up the stages of moral reasoning is the inevitable result. They are also experimenting with building "just communities" in schools, to help students learn to apply to principles of justice, reciprocity, and so on in a naturalistic setting.

Other educators intervene in the cognitive and decision-making areas by teaching students analytical and critical-thinking skills (for example, Raths *et al.*, 1967) and the structure of logical and/or decision-making skills, all of which are essential for more effective personal and social choices.

Common Ground Among Values-Education Approaches

Other specific approaches to values education could be mentioned, and a great deal of time could be spent contrasting each and every one of them. I find it more useful at this point to consider what they have in common, for in that area of overlap I see the possibility of some clarity about future directions in values education. It seems to me that the various values-education approaches that are being taken most seriously today and used most widely have several things in common.

First, they try to teach young people (and adults) a set of *valuing skills* or *valuing processes*. The concept of skills is very useful, I think, because we are on secure ground in communicating with educators and the community if we refer to that widely accepted function of schools—teaching pupils skills. Therefore, if we could take from each of the values-education approaches those skills that seem critical to the development of personally satisfying and socially constructive living, I think we would really have something important—a set of specific objectives for values education that could be agreed upon and measured.

I have previously (Kirschenbaum, 1973) tried to formulate such a list of valuing skills, representing those skills or processes emphasized by the various approaches mentioned earlier and some from approaches like Effectiveness Training (Gordon, 1970, 1975) and Reevaluation Counseling (Jackins, 1965) that have not yet been cited. The skills cluster under what I would call the five "dimensions" of the overall valuing process:

Thinking

1. On many levels (for example, Bloom, Englehart, Furst, Walker, and Krathwohl, 1956)
2. Critical thinking (for example, Raths, Wasserman, Jonas, and Rothstein, 1967; Metcalf, 1971)
3. Divergent, creative thinking (for example, Parnes, 1967)
4. Moral reasoning (for example, Kohlberg, 1968)

Feeling

5. Being aware of one's feelings (for example, Rogers, 1961)
6. Dealing with distressful feelings (Jackins, 1965)
7. Experiencing positive self-esteem (for example, Norem-Hebeisen, 1976)

Choosing or Decision-Making

8. Goal-setting
9. Data-gathering
10. Choosing from alternatives (Raths *et al.,* 1966)
11. Choosing after considering consequences (Raths *et al.,* 1966)
12. Choosing freely (Raths *et al.,* 1966)
13. Soliciting feedback about the results

Communicating

14. Sending clear messages (for example, Gordon, 1970)
15. Empathic listening (for example, Gordon, 1970; Rogers, 1951)
16. "No-lose" conflict resolution (for example, Gordon, 1970)

Acting

17. Acting skillfully, competently, including: (a) academic skills, (b) professional skills, (c) personal-social skills.

These dimensions of the valuing process overlap; they are not discrete psychological processes. For example, one may be thinking, communicating, and acting simultaneously. The skills or processes are not necessarily used in the order in which they are presented here —that depends upon the context and the person. Finally, this list is not meant to be definitive. Depending upon our own orientation, we might add or delete a given skill or use different terms.

The listing, then, is not the product of any one school of thought, but an integration of many approaches to values education. Based on the separate theories of each school represented and on the research each has conducted, I suggest that it is possible to state the following as the main hypothesis of values education: *The consistent, skillful, and appropriate use of these valuing processes increases the likelihood that our choices and living will have value for ourselves and be constructive in the social context.* This would imply that the entire field of values education can be clarified toward the objective of teaching a definable set of skills.

As a part of teaching the various valuing skills, different approaches provide students with *practice* in using the skills and applying them to values-laden areas in their lives. Sometimes the practice uses abstract issues or moral dilemmas distant from students' immediate concerns. This would be true of the original Kohlberg model and occasionally of the values-analysis model. Approaches like values clarification and the Rucker *et al.* (1969) model tend to give students practice using the valuing skills by having them think about and discuss and act on real issues in their lives, for instance, family, friends, school, leisure time, and the like. All the approaches are amenable to being used with socially important content—economics, racism, energy, male-female roles, and so on. In any case, the goal is the same —to reinforce the skills that have been learned or that are being learned, and to encourage students to apply the skills across the range of human experience, including their own lives.

Another thing that many of the approaches have in common is the creation of discrepancies or dissonance in the person's thinking, intended as a step toward value and moral development. Values clarification puts great emphasis on exposing students to alternative belief and action models. Moral developmentalists stress the importance of exposing students to levels of moral reasoning one stage above their own. Rokeach (1973) highlights the dissonance created when experimental subjects find that a reference group they admire has responded differently than they did to a similar values survey. Each of these approaches postulates, explicitly or implicitly, that such an exposure to alternative frames of reference contributes to a positive change in values or level of moral reasoning. The research of any one of these schools of thought could be used to help explain the methodology of the other schools. There seems to be a developing consistency in our understanding of how values develop and change.

So where are we in values education? To summarize the previous discussion, we have a number of approaches, each with its own theoretical base, materials, methods, and research support. Most eschew any attempt to inculcate specific values regarding religion, politics, and the like, but they are not value-free. Implicitly or explicity, they affirm certain values consistent with a democratic philosophy. I have suggested that there are two key values or goals these approaches have in common. First is the inalienable right of each person to a personally fulfilling life—"life" and "the pursuit of happiness," as Jefferson phrased it in the Declaration of Independence. Second are the principles of freedom, justice, and equality—in a word, "liberty." The founders of this country stated simply that these truths or values were "self-evident." We can do more than that today. There is a tradition now in psychological research (for example, Kohlberg, 1969; Rogers, 1964) that suggests that these values are also natural or universal. That is no ultimate proof of their desirability, but it adds credence to the growing number of educational approaches that are aimed at equipping students with the skills and attitudes necessary to the fulfillment of Jefferson's dream.

Where Do We Go From Here?

Beginning with John Dewey, the concern with citizenship education has played an important part in the language of modern pedagogy. The recent renaissance in values education is a continuation of that tradition, based on a firmer base of psychological theory and research. But in many ways, we are still only at the beginning stages of development in this area.

We might look at two areas of future effort: (a) research and development, that is, the generation of new knowledge and technique, and (b) dissemination, that is, the implementation on a broad scale of the best knowledge and techniques presently available.

Research

I see the need for two kinds of research and development in this area—what I would call (a) specific and (b) integrative.

Specific research and development efforts would be aimed at helping the most promising approaches to values education continue their good work. Approaches like values clarification, moral development, values analysis, and others are worthy of further support because they are consistent with democratic educational goals, they have some empirical research base, and they have demonstrated the ability to appeal to large segments of the population. In other words, people use these approaches; they affect the lives of children. Each of these schools has important concerns that should be pursued: At what grade levels is a given approach more effective? What kinds of students do or do not profit from certain approaches or certain kinds of interventions? What teacher-training models in a given approach lead to the greatest positive change in the teachers' and students' behavior? And so on. The specific approaches should be enabled to separately pursue these kinds of questions, thereby generating new information on the nature of values and moral development and the means of influencing it in public education.

This is not to say that each and every proposal using the words values, morals, or the like should be funded. Personally, I have been asked to consult with many values-education projects seeking funding. When I examined some of the proposals, I felt that these projects would add little that was new in terms of research or development. Such funds might provide needed teacher training in a given district, but I question whether in the long run that money will have been spent wisely. There is certainly room for valid disagreement among people in the field as to what research should or should not be funded; I would simply caution that we have considerable knowledge about values education at this point and rather than continue to reinvent the wheel, we should be willing to fund less pedestrian projects that might have far-reaching consequences. Why not, for example, go to some of the leaders in the different values education approaches who have distinguished themselves and ask, "If you had x number of dollars to explore any questions which you think are critical in your area, what would you propose?" I venture to say that out of that would come some ideas that might lead to noteworthy research efforts in American education.

In any event, developmental work in the separate approaches should go forward, even to the point of funding entire schools to be set up according to the educational philosophy of the various values education models, with the results, problems, and successes carefully monitored.

A second type of needed research, in my opinion, would be integrative in nature. It would frequently be longitudinal. Let me give two examples.

If two common goals of values education are, in fact, the achievement of a personally satisfying life and socially constructive behavior, we might find or create the instruments best suited to measuring those two phenomena. We might then form a variety of experimental groups and provide each with an educational experience over several years that utilizes a particular values-education approach. Such an experiment could tell us which approaches are more effective for what ends, what kinds of students work best with which approaches, and the like. It would both increase our knowledge about values growth and development and provide an important validity check on the claims made by the individual values approaches.

Another kind of integrative research effort would be to examine more closely the array of valuing skills I identified earlier in this article. Again, we could identify or create the instruments that would best measure the individual's skill in utilizing each valuing process. This would enable us to distinguish the "high valuing person" (the one who thinks critically, chooses from alternatives, and so on) from the "low valuing person" (the one who does not distinguish fact from opinion, chooses the first alternative which comes along, and so on). An enormous amount of significant data could be derived from a cross-sectional study of thousands of people, of all ages, races, economic and other backgrounds, measuring their degree of valuing skills and correlating this factor with job and life satisfaction, citizenship behaviors (do they vote or write letters to the editor?), health, family adjustment, and so on. Are the valuing skills correlated with "success" for all people or just for some ages, races, and so on? Are all the valuing skills important, are only selected skills important, or are some skills more important than others? Will a factor analysis show that each valuing skill is a distinct factor or that there are some groupings that would allow us to combine several of the valuing skills into one category and thereby clarify even further the specific skills we want to aim for in values education? The possibilities are endless.

What I am suggesting is that we need to back away a bit from some of the narrower specific questions and tackle some of the biggest and most important questions in values education, questions that transcend any specific values-education approach; in other words, questions like: What would the product of an ideal values/moral education look like and how can we best achieve that kind of result?

I sometimes wonder if there is not a fear among funding sources to tackle this kind of a task. It probably seems much safer to fund 10 different projects for $100,000 than one project for 1 million dollars—safer politically and safer in the sense that with 10 projects, somebody is bound to come up with something worthwhile, but with one project, you never know. I suggest that one well-selected larger project might, in the long run, take us further than 10 projects that are smaller or narrower in scope. Fortunately, it is not an either-or situation. Both kinds of projects deserve support. Still, I think that more daring is necessary in funding projects that can demonstrate almost conclusively some major premises about values education and thereby focus all our work in even more productive directions for years to come.

Dissemination

While this kind of research goes on, we need to do the best we can with the knowledge we have. How do we inform the largest number of educators about better values-education materials and methods that are currently available?

Demonstration schools using the different values education approaches are one method. Such schools can expose thousands of visiting educators to concrete examples of important educational models. This also would be consistent with the current funding programs supporting schools and centers that demonstrate promising approaches.

Three other dissemination approaches constitute the three major programs of my own organization—the National Humanistic Education Center. These programs are teacher training, development of materials, and establishment of support groups. Let me explain these.

It has been my experience that teachers and administrators primarily develop a commitment to values education of the kind I have been describing when they have actively participated in a workshop, class, or learning experience. In other words, only when educators experience a concrete example of such an approach and realize what a satisfying learning experience it can be do they become motivated to change their teaching behavior significantly in this direction. All school district policy statements include references to moral or citizenship education; but it is so hard to effect competently that most people steer clear of it.

Funds for teacher training in this area help encourage these kinds of learning experiences. Better still would be to set up some kind of system whereby funds would be made available for the training of in-house trainers. Districts could be paid for sending teachers or administrators (volunteers) to, let us say, a regional workshop if the districts make a commitment to having these teachers or administrators return to conduct further training in the district.

Films of some of the major values-education approaches in operation in real classrooms would be an excellent aid to disseminating our present methods on a wide scale. These could become an important part of in-service training and loaned to districts across the country at minimal expense. Media Five Films (3211 Cahuenga Boulevard West, Hollywood, California 90068), for example, has an excellent twelve-part series on the values clarification and moral development approaches.

In the area of materials for education, there has been a great deal written in the field of values education. Superka, Johnson, and Ahrens (1975) have provided one model for analyzing materials in the field. Our Center is compiling a catalogue of materials for teachers that show how to teach the valuing skills and deal with values issues in specific subject areas like English, history, math, and science. We have found in the past that when we publish such listings, drawing together all the materials available in one source, thousands of districts, schools, and individual teachers write in for the materials. Would it be too commercial to suggest that an agency like the National Institute of Education set up, or contract with a nonprofit organization to set up a clearinghouse to make available, at cost, the best and most useful materials in the field of values education? I do not mean a complete listing of everything that has been written in the field, with a long computer print-out that provides persons with little or no guidance in their choices. I mean a narrower selection of the most practical materials that teachers can use to implement the values-education approaches. Our Center has had a great deal of success with this approach, and I see no reason why it could not be implemented on a wider scale.

The third dissemination approach that we are using at the National Humanistic Education Center is that of support groups. We have written a *Manual for Professional Support Groups* (Kirschenbaum and Glaser, 1976) and are now fieldtesting it in several localities. Our hypothesis is that self-help peer, professional-learning, and support groups can become potent cost-effective vehicles for helping disseminate promising approaches, for facilitating educators learning about new methods from each other, and for providing the emotional and professional support that innovators so often need.

These dissemination approaches have great potential, I think, for reaching a wide audience of educators across the country. Many have been used in other areas, for example, individualized instruction and career education. They could readily be used in the field of values, moral, and citizenship education.

Community Reaction

How does the community at large react to all this? I have suggested that most values educators, if they could separate themselves a bit from their vested interests in their own approaches, can agree on broad goals and specific objectives for values education. Are most parents, religious leaders, and community members ready to go along?

I do not know of extensive research that really answers this question, although many surveys have been done. Questionnaires given to parents and others often tend to reflect the biases of the surveyor because of the way the questions are asked. If we were to ask persons, "Do you believe the schools have a responsibility in helping children become good citizens?" or "Do you believe that schools should help give students the skills to build personally satisfying lives and be constructive members of society?" it is obvious that the vast majority respond favorably. If, on the other hand, we ask, "Do you think schools should take on the responsibility that was previously left to the home and the church, that of teaching values?" it is clear that most would answer negatively. So questionnaire data on community opinion must be viewed very cautiously; in my experience, it is almost always motivated by and used as political strategy for someone or some group wanting to implement their own philosophy.

My opinion on community reaction to values education is that parents, religious leaders, and others sincerely desire the broad goals of values education mentioned earlier. They want children to lead purposeful, satisfying lives, and they want them to be constructive members of the community. They also want children to have the valuing skills to obtain these two broad objectives. However, when certain controversial issues are involved, some members of the community prefer that their children not be exposed to certain points of view or not be exposed to the issues at all. Such exposure, they feel, threatens their own authority and could be harmful to the children.

I hasten to point out that this rarely becomes a major problem for values education. Normally values educators use common sense about possible or actual community reaction. By using good taste and by occasionally avoiding controversial issues that are certain to create strong feelings and polarization, the overall values-education program is allowed to continue intact. In cases where individual parents are strongly against their children's participation in certain aspects of the values education program, opportunities for alternative learning experiences can be provided. Adequate teacher preparation, administrative support, and continuing emphasis on basic academic skills will all help ensure the longevity of the program. With this kind of responsible implementation, the majority of parents respond positively to values education. The approach I am most familiar with, values clarification, has been implemented, I would estimate, in thousands of districts across the country. I find it significant that I have heard of relatively few incidents where it became a source of serious community controversy.

In the small minority of cases where there is vigorous community opposition to values education, the schools are faced with a dilemma not unique to values education. Who ultimately controls the schools? Parents, taxpayers, teachers, administrators, students, school boards, and even the courts each make some claim to a decision-making role. Until these problems are resolved by society as a whole, then values education—like busing, school financing, community control, segregation, and other issues—will be merely the battleground on which a more basic issue is fought.

In most districts, however, values education will continue to be more like most educational innovations. Can it be supported on its merits? Can it win adherents? Can it continue to survive and flourish, or will it go the way of other educational fads and panaceas? I think we have the evidence to show that values education is more than a fad; it is supported by a growing base of sound theory and research and, more important, is crucial for the well-being of our society.

B. S. Bloom, M. D. Englehart, E. J. Furst, H. H. Walker, and D. R. Krathwohl. *The Taxonomy of Educational Objectives: Handbook I: The Cognitive Domain.* New York: McKay, 1956.

T. Gordon. *Parent Effectiveness Training*. New York: Peter Wyden, 1970.

T. Gordon. *Teacher Effectiveness Training*. New York: Peter Wyden, 1975.

M. Harmin, H. Kirschenbaum, and S. B. Simon. *Clarifying Values Through Subject Matter*. Minneapolis: Winston, 1973.

H. Jackins. *The Human Side of Human Beings*. Seattle: Rational Island Publishers, 1965.

H. Kirschenbaum. *Advanced Values Clarification*. La Jolla, California: University Associates, 1977.

H. Kirschenbaum. "Beyond Values Clarification." *Humanistic Education Quarterly,* 2(3):1-19; 1973.

H. Kirschenbaum and B. Glaser. *Manual for Professional Support Groups*. Saratoga Springs, New York: National Humanistic Education Center, 1976.

H. Kirschenbaum, M. Harmin, L. Howe, and S. B. Simon. *In Defense of Values Clarification: A Position Paper*. Occasional paper. Saratoga Springs, New York: National Humanistic Education Center, 1975.

L. Kohlberg. "Stage and Sequence: The Cognitive-Developmental Approach to Socialization." See: D. Goslin, editor. *Handbook of Socialization Theory and Research*. New York: Rand-McNally, 1969.

L. Kohlberg. "The Child as a Moral Philosopher." *Psychology Today* 7:25-30; 1968.

R. Larson and D. Larson. *Values and Faith*. Minneapolis: Winston, 1976.

H. Laswell. *The World Revolution of Our Time*. Stanford, California: Stanford University Press, 1951.

L. E. Metcalf, editor. *Values Education: Rationale, Strategies and Procedures*. Washington, D.C.: National Council for the Social Studies, 1971.

A. Norem-Hebeisen. *Exploring your Self-esteem: Teachers Guide to the Self-assessment Scales*. Saratoga Spring, New York: National Humanistic Education Center, 1976.

S. J. Parnes. *Creative Behavior Guidebook*. New York: Scribners, 1967.

L. Raths, M. Harmin, and S. B. Simon. *Values and Teaching*. Columbus, Ohio: Merrill, 1966.

L. E. Raths, S. Wasserman, A. Jonas, and A. M. Rothstein. *Teacher for Thinking*. Columbus, Ohio: Merrill, 1967.

C. R. Rogers. *Client-centered Therapy*. Boston: Houghton Mifflin, 1951.

C. R. Rogers. *On Becoming a Person*. Boston: Houghton Mifflin, 1961.

C. R. Rogers. "Toward a Modern Approach to Values: The Valuing Process in the Mature Person." *Journal of Abnormal and Social Psychology* 68 (2) :160-167: 1964.

M. Rokeach. *The Nature of Human Values*. New York: Free Press, 1973.

M. Rokeach. "Toward a Philosophy of Value Education." See: J. Meyer, B. Burnahm, and J. Cholvat, editors. *Values Education: Theory, Practice, Problems, Prospects*. Waterloo, Ontario: Wilfred Laurier University Press, 1975.

W. Rucker, V. C. Arnspiger, and A. J. Brodbeck. *Human Values in Education*. Dubuque, Iowa: Wm. C. Brown, 1969.

S. B. Simon, L. Howe, and H. Kirschenbaum. *Values Clarification: A Handbook of Practical Strategies for Teachers and Students*. New York: Hart Publishing, 1972.

D. Superka, P. Johnson, and C. Ahrens. *Values Education: Approaches and Materials*. Boulder, Colorado: Social Science Education Consortium and ERIC Clearinghouse for Social Studies, Social Science Education, 1975.

Contributors to This Booklet

R. FREEMAN BUTTS, Dean, School of Education, San José State University, San Jose, California.

DONALD H. PECKENPAUGH, Superintendent, Birmingham Public Schools, Birmingham, Michigan.

HOWARD KIRSCHENBAUM, Director, National Humanistic Education Center, Saratoga Springs, New York.

LOUIS J. RUBIN, Professor of Education, University of Illinois, Urbana.

ASCD Publications, Autumn 1977

Yearbooks

Education for an Open Society (610-74012)	$8.00
Education for Peace: Focus on Mankind (610-17946)	$7.50
Evaluation as Feedback and Guide (610-17700)	$6.50
Feeling, Valuing, and the Art of Growing: Insights into the Affective (610-77104)	$9.75
Freedom, Bureaucracy, & Schooling (610-17508)	$6.50
Learning and Mental Health in the School (610-17674)	$5.00
Life Skills in School and Society (610-17786)	$5.50
A New Look at Progressive Education (610-17812)	$8.00
Perspectives on Curriculum Development 1776-1976 (610-76078)	$9.50
Schools in Search of Meaning (610-75044)	$8.50
Perceiving, Behaving, Becoming: A New Focus for Education (610-17278)	$5.00
To Nurture Humaneness: Commitment for the '70's (610-17810)	$6.00

Books and Booklets

Action Learning: Student Community Service Projects (611-74018)	$2.50
Adventuring, Mastering, Associating: New Strategies for Teaching Children (611-76080)	$5.00
Beyond Jencks: The Myth of Equal Schooling (611-17928)	$2.00
The Changing Curriculum: Mathematics (611-17724)	$2.00
Criteria for Theories of Instruction (611-17756)	$2.00
Curricular Concerns in a Revolutionary Era (611-17852)	$6.00
Curriculum Leaders: Improving Their Influence (611-76084)	$4.00
Curriculum Theory (611-77112)	$7.00
Degrading the Grading Myths: A Primer of Alternatives to Grades and Marks (611-76082)	$6.00
Differentiated Staffing (611-17924)	$3.50
Discipline for Today's Children and Youth (611-17314)	$1.50
Educational Accountability: Beyond Behavioral Objectives (611-17856)	$2.50
Elementary School Mathematics: A Guide to Current Research (611-75056)	$5.00
Elementary School Science: A Guide to Current Research (611-17726)	$2.25
Eliminating Ethnic Bias in Instructional Materials: Comment and Bibliography (611-74020)	$3.25
Emerging Moral Dimensions in Society: Implications for Schooling (611-75052)	$3.75
Ethnic Modification of Curriculum (611-17832)	$1.00
Global Studies: Problems and Promises for Elementary Teachers (611-76086)	$4.50
The Humanities and the Curriculum (611-17708)	$2.00
Impact of Decentralization on Curriculum: Selected Viewpoints (611-75050)	$3.75
Improving Educational Assessment & An Inventory of Measures of Affective Behavior (611-17804)	$4.50
International Dimension of Education (611-17816)	$2.25
Interpreting Language Arts Research for the Teacher (611-17846)	$4.00
Learning More About Learning (611-17310)	$2.00
Linguistics and the Classroom Teacher (611-17720)	$2.75
A Man for Tomorrow's World (611-17838)	$2.25
Middle School in the Making (611-74024)	$5.00
The Middle School We Need (611-75060)	$2.50
Multicultural Education: Commitments, Issues, and Applications (611-77108)	$7.00
Needs Assessment: A Focus for Curriculum Development (611-75048)	$4.00
Observational Methods in the Classroom (611-17948)	$3.50
Open Education: Critique and Assessment (611-75054)	$4.75
Open Schools for Children (611-17916)	$3.75
Professional Supervision for Professional Teachers (611-75046)	$4.50
Removing Barriers to Humaneness in the High School (611-17848)	$2.50
Reschooling Society: A Conceptual Model (611-17950)	$2.00
The School of the Future—NOW (611-17920)	$3.75
Schools Become Accountable: A PACT Approach (611-74016)	$3.50
The School's Role as Moral Authority (611-77110)	$4.50
Social Studies for the Evolving Individual (611-17952)	$3.00
Staff Development: Staff Liberation (611-77106)	$6.50
Supervision: Emerging Profession (611-17796)	$5.00
Supervision in a New Key (611-17926)	$2.50
Supervision: Perspectives and Propositions (611-17732)	$2.00
What Are the Sources of the Curriculum? (611-17522)	$1.50
Vitalizing the High School (611-74026)	$3.50
Developmental Characteristics of Children and Youth (wall chart) (611-75058)	$2.00

Discounts on quantity orders of same title to single address: 10-49 copies, 10%; 50 or more copies, 15%. Make checks or money orders payable to ASCD. Orders totaling $10.00 or less must be prepaid. Orders from institutions and businesses must be on official purchase order form. Shipping and handling charges will be added to billed purchase orders. **Please be sure to list the stock number of each publication, shown in parentheses.**

Subscription to **Educational Leadership**—$10.00 a year. ASCD Membership dues: Regular (subscription and yearbook)—$25.00 a year; Comprehensive (includes subscription and yearbook plus other books and booklets distributed during period of membership)—$35.00 a year.

Order from: **Association for Supervision and Curriculum Development**
Suite 1100, 1701 K Street, N.W., Washington, D.C. 20006